Ed Parker's

INFINITE INSIGHTS *INTO* KENPO
INSIGHTS

VOLUME 3

PHYSICAL ANALYZATION II

by

ED PARKER

All Rights Reserved
Printed in the United States of America
Library of Congress Card Number 82-72784
First Printing July, 1985

ISBN 0910293-10-4 (5 Volume Set)
ISBN 0910293-05-8 (Volume 3 - cloth)
ISBN 0910293-04-X (Volume 3 - paper)

DELSBY PUBLICATIONS
Los Angeles, California

TABLE OF CONTENTS

ACKNOWLEDGEMENTS iii
DEDICATION iv
PLEDGES v
ABOUT THE PLEDGES vi
PREFACE vii
CHAPTER 1 -- INTRODUCTION 1
CHAPTER 2 -- DIVISION OF THE BASICS 3
    a. Organizational Chart on Basics 4
CHAPTER 3 -- BLOCKS 5
    a. Organizational Chart on Blocks 7
      1) Blocks With the Hand and Arm 10
        a) Striking 10
        b) Parrying 35
        c) Positioned 47
        d) Pinning 50
        e) Specialized 53
      2) Blocks With the Foot and Leg 62
        a) Striking 62
        b) Parrying 67
        c) Positioned 71
CHAPTER 4 -- STRIKES 73
    a. Organizational Chart on Strikes 79
      1) Strikes With the and Hand Arm 80
        a) Clawing 80
        b) Slicing 91
        c) Whipping 95
        d) Thrusting 97
        e) Hooking 102
        f) Roundhousing 105
        g) Hammering 108
        h) Specialized 112
      2) A Comparative Analysis of the Arms and
        Legs 116
      3) Concept of Minor and Major Moves 121
      4) Determining Factors 124

5) Strikes With the Foot and Leg 127
    a) Slicing 127
    b) Whipping 133
    c) Thrusting 137
        (1) Angle of No Return 142
    d) Hooking 144
        (1) Front Scoop Kick 146
    e) Roundhousing 151
    f) Hammering 154
    g) Specialized 158
6) Strikes With the Head 164
7) A Composite of Natural Weapons 168

CHAPTER 5 -- SPECIALIZED MOVES AND METHODS 169
    a. Organizational Chart on Specialized Moves and Methods 171

CHAPTER 6 -- EXERCISES 177
    a. Pre--Stretching 177
    b. Other Exercises Conducive to Leg Training 190
    1) Stretching 190
    2) Strengthening 192

CHAPTER 7 -- CONCLUSION 199

GLOSSARY OF TERMINOLOGY . . . . x i

ACKNOWLEDGEMENTS

Teamwork is the key in making any project a success. Without the cooperative efforts of others, projects are often left to lay dormant for years, or in some cases, never see fruition.

The greatest reward in the completion of this as well as the remaining two volumes is the result of allowing associates the responsibility and freedom of being creative without interference. Instituting this philosophy has given this volume a more professional appearance. I am grateful to Jim Grunwald's photographic skills and my son Edmund's graphic artwork whose creativity excells with each volume, my wife, Leilani, for her patience in editing my manuscripts, Arnold Inouye for catching many of my spelling errors, my daughter Sheri for her artistic touches; to my brother David whose drawings appear profusely throughout these volumes, to Fred Stille for his constructive comments and suggestions, and to Frank Trejo who spent untold hours posing for this and the remaining volumes that complete this series. I also thank Paul Girard, Khatchik (Chris) Yeressian, Ron Chapel, Galu Tafua, Ed Booze, James Lowell, and Joe Kowalik for their patience in posing for photographs, and Craig L. Weidel for his contributions regarding pre-stretching exercises. To many others who directly or indirectly helped with the creation of my five volume series, I also express my deep gratitude.

Skip Hancock and Shawn Gants were extremely helpful in making it possible to meet my printer's deadline. Their around the clock assistance is also deserving of my thanks.

While the names of those who have helped go on and on, I feel compelled to conclude by expressing my gratitude to Howard Silva. He has not only helped me pose for this volume, but has been an inspiration to those young practitioners whom he has contact with. Men like him are responsible for prodding others to continue their training in Kenpo.

DEDICATION

I dedicate this volume to Bernie Bernheim, deceased, whose unselfish efforts to share the Art of Kenpo with others was unmatched. His unceasing interest and encouragement has been instrumental in my desire to complete the remainder of my five volume series. I know he supports me in spirit that I, too, share my knowledge of Kenpo with those who are willing to learn.

PLEDGES

ORANGE BELT PLEDGE - I understand that I am but a beginner in a new and fascinating art which will direct me to greater obligations and responsibilities. To honor my obligations and responsibilities I pledge myself to serve my instructor, fellow students, and fellow men.

PURPLE BELT PLEDGE - I hold the art of Kenpo sacred and freely take upon myself the obligation and responsibility that I shall never misuse my skill to hurt or make afraid. I shall fight only if forced to defend myself and shall be slow to anger, loath to take offense, quick to forgive, and to forget personal affront.

BLUE BELT PLEDGE - I shall never let pride rule my passions and will defend, with all the skill I possess, the weak, the helpless, and the oppressed. I pledge an unswerving loyalty to the Association and my instructor. In addition, I pledge an unending effort to earn the self-same loyalty from those who look to me for training.

GREEN BELT PLEDGE - I pledge a continued effort to sharpen my skills, to increase my knowledge, and to broaden my horizons. I shall obligate myself under the direction of my instructor to learn the skills of a teacher which will enable me to teach my skills in the prescribed manner outlined by Mr. Ed Parker.

ABOUT THE PLEDGES

The pledges in this volume are extensions of the CREED, composed and designed to further promulgate spiritual character among the lower ranks -- Orange Belt to Green Belt. As extensions, they, too, denote the Martial Artist's way of life in today's environment and, therefore, also act as a regulatory guide in aiding the Martial Artist in developing a keen sense of justice. As students progress through the three levels of Brown Belt, their spiritual and character building resposibilities are proportionately increased through further pledge commitments listed in Volume IV. At the time that they become First Degree Black Belts, they must again take the final pledge (see Volume V) in order to enter the realm of the Fraternal Order of Black Belts.

PREFACE

It has been nearly 30 years since Ed Parker brought Kenpo to the mainland United States. In that time, much has been said both positively and negatively about this patriarch and his system. While disciples praise his system as being highly effective, the ultimate in self-defense; others label the system as no more than sophisticated streetfighting or downgrade it as an overcomplicated "slap art". Regardless of what has been said by both supporters and detractors, the fact remains -- the man stands alone as a genius in the modern day science of self-defense. Unfortunately, like other fields of endeavor, public acceptance of living artists is seldom achieved. The general pattern is to wait until great artists are dead before acknowledging their invaluable contributions. There are, fortunately, a few instances where they are recognized and accepted while they are still alive. Such is true of Ed Parker. Many of us feel privileged to be constituents of his *infinite* knowledge of the Martial Arts. As a student and disciple, I can state that he is unquestionably the Master of *American Kenpo.*

Mr. Parker's life ambition has been to expand the scope of the Arts, and, therefore, his list of firsts is long. One need only look back over the years, referencing books and articles he has written, articles that have been written about him or crediting him, to verify this fact. However, Mr. Parker has not only been misquoted, but also misinterpreted which has resulted in unwarranted controversy. There has been an ongoing argument among some Martial Artists about the person who should be called the "Father of American Karate"? The title was given to Ed Parker in an article written about him in a magazine -- he did not claim it. He also does not claim to have opened the first Karate school in the United States. His claim is to have opened the first *official commercial* school, in Provo, Utah in 1954. Regarding Martial Arts *clubs,* they probably existed for over 50 years before there were any formed by Americans. Chinese immigrants who were brought to the United States in the 1800's practiced their Art at that time. As Tongs (syndicates) were formed Martial Arts Masters were hired to tutor their members. Although membership was restricted to Chinese, Martial Arts, nevertheless, flourished within their *clubs.*

As referred to earlier, an accusation made by persons unfamiliar with Kenpo is that it is a "slap art". That is, they wrongfully believe that *slaps* are inserted in a technique sequence to create sound effects rather than effectiveness. The "slap art" label stems from practitioners and observers alike who have not been privileged to analytically study the details involved in a technique. Consequently some moves are mistaken for a *slap.* To compound this misconception less experienced students often improperly imitate their instructor. The truth of the matter is that many Kenpo techniques employ open hand *checks.* These *checks* insure the prevention of retaliatory moves (anticipated and unexpected) on the part of the opponent, or in some cases, act as a brace to enhance the effectiveness of your action. There are a number of methods used to check an opponent's actions -- *striking checks, parrying checks, pinning checks, bracing checks, positioned checks,* etc. Once the *check* is determined the slap is then visibly executed in a technique to indicate, by touch and sound, where the *check* is to be inserted. Only when the physical action of a check is rendered will you know the true value of these *checks.*

Interestingly enough, there was a letter written to a magazine years ago commenting on the slap. This letter caused an avalanche of mail. Ironically the very same man who criticized Kenpo, labelling it a "Slap art", recently attended a seminar by Ed Parker in Chicago. He admitted writing the letter and confessed that at the time, he did not understand the Kenpo System. He apologized to Mr. Parker personally and added that the seminar had made him realize he was mistaken.

Other critics have said that Kenpo practitioners employ "overkill" tactics. Not being aware of what we are doing, they have felt that many of our moves are unnecessary. Kenpo's lengthy self-defense techniques are designed to anticipate expected, as well as, unexpected reactions. This concept allows you room for error in combat. Students are programmed with a variety of strikes and checks for the purpose of insuring survival in an altercation. However, Kenpo techniques do not rely on cumulative impacts. Karate's theory of the "one punch kill" does parallel the Kenpo philosophy. We, too, believe that we can drop an opponent with one shot utilizing maximum power resulting in a minimum of exposure. But Kenpo differs in its approach -- it is much more realistic. Misses are contemplated. At times counters can be ineffective, thus requiring follow-up techniques. Unexpected reactions can cause defeat. For these reasons as well as others Kenpo provides knowledge of "how to" react from all positions and angles in expected as well as unexpected situations. It exposes a student to a variety of methods of executing weapons (natural or otherwise), angles of delivery, combination counters, etc. *while checking.* Part of Kenpo education is to *feel* in order to believe. Not until these *checks* are applied to you do you feel, recognize, and acknowledge their use and value.

Kenpo can be passive as well as aggressive, which is a surprise to many who brand Kenpo as solely aggressive. Kenpo's all encompassing knowledge of motion allows for tremendous latitude and flexibility. Any degree of force or restraint can be executed. It is often the predicament that determines your choice of action. If it is a life or death situation the extent of injury is regulated accordingly. If it is a drunk meaning no harm the action taken is one of restraint and humiliation. The philosophy of Kenpo is to parallel the predicament to the degree of danger imposed. However, regardless of the magnitude of the attack, we avoid death when retaliating.

Finally, it has been said that Kenpo is too technical. That is, it is too wrapped up in concepts and terminology. The question then is why are concepts and terminology applied to other sciences? The answer is simple -- these terms further refine and define the intricacies involved in the particular science studied. Ed Parker has created terminology that specifically and pictorially describes the concepts and actions of Kenpo. The terms often literally gives one a mental picture of the concepts or moves being learned. The effects of relating movements to terms, or vice versa, not only speeds up the learning process, but enhances retention as well. While some of these terms have scientific roots similar to math and physics, Ed Parker has created new terms which were non-existent in the Martial Arts. His expanded glossary resulted from introducing new concepts in this highly developed Martial Arts science. Fortunately, many of these concepts and terms can be found in all five volumes of "Infinite Insights into Kenpo". This volume is only one of five volumes that reveals much of the discoveries and experiences developed by the Master of our system, Ed Parker.

Not only is it my privilege to write the preface to this volume, it is my pleasure as well to study under Mr. Parker. From time to time I have had opportunities to work with other well known Martial Artists. On numerous occasions, they have imparted what they have termed "new techniques". To my amazement I discovered that these same techniques were standard practices in Kenpo and the basic ingredients of an all encompassing system. Although this knowledge was a pleasant surprise it further strengthens my faith in the man and his system.

Lee Wedlake Jr.

CHAPTER 1
INTRODUCTION

Volume III is a continued segment of Volume II. It, too, has been structured to create interest in viewing related facets of the Martial Arts from new and varied perspectives. While both Volumes technically describe the BASIC fundamentals in the five major categories that comprise *American* Kenpo, Volume III is specifically concerned with BLOCKS, STRIKES, and SPECIALIZED MOVES AND METHODS.

Emphasis is again placed on utilizing the *principle of tailoring* -- a principle that stresses the need to *tailor* (see Volume V, Chapter 3) BASIC fundamentals of your physical make-up. Applying this principle helps to solidify balance as well as increase speed, power, and accuracy. Combine the BASICS described in this Volume with the STANCES and MANEUVERS already learned in Volume II and you will increase the effectiveness of your actions beyond expectation.

"Man is a tool-using animal. Without tools, he is nothing; with tools he is all." -- is so true. To go one step further, "A man who has comprehensive knowledge of *principles* and *knows how to apply them* when he uses his tools, adds greater impetus to the word 'all'". *Principles* are the keys which allow man to use his tools properly and effectively. With a comprehensive knowledge of *principles* (see Volume IV, Chapter 7), maximum benefits can be derived. Partial knowledge only deterres the efforts expended. Although the statement, "Inconsistency is the only thing in which men are consistent.", may occasionally hold true, Martial Artists must be *consistent* with their use of *principles*. Although *there is no right way to do a wrong thing*, the more *consistent* you become in applying *correct principles*, the closer you will come to executing moves the *right way*. It must be realized, however, that the *right way* differs among individuals. *Correct principles* should be applied according to an individual's physical make-up. It is only after the proper diagnosis is determined that the *correct principles* can be prescribed in maximizing an individual's efforts. As each formula is prescribed for the physical make-up of the individual concerned, the *right way* becomes automatic and surprisingly *consistent*.

The intelligent man is one who has successfully fulfilled many accomplishments and yet is still willing to learn more. He knows that the future belongs to those who prepare for it. He lives by the law that "There is no reward without *work* being expended...each day is a new day, an opportunity for a new beginning". *Work* to him goes on now as well as tomorrow, not yesterday, for he understands that "procrastination is the art of keeping up with yesterday". He looks upon *work* as a challenge, not a chore; a blessing, not a bore. As a result, he knows that *work* is not meant to be a penalty for living, but a reward for accomplishment. He firmly believes that the only time success comes before work is found in the dictionary. He realizes that the difference between *knowing of a subject* and *knowing a subject* comes through the intelligent use of time. Knowing the value of time makes him appreciate *work*. Although he exercises patience, he is careful not to *overwork* it. He is cognizant that *study* and *work* allows him greater boundaries that free him from following nonsensical rules. He fully understands that rules are often made for those who's brainpower runs out.   He realizes that he doesn't know all of the answers because he has not heard all of the questions. He accepts the saying..."know what you know; know why it's so". While others are trying to *better themselves* he knows that the real answer lies in making *themselves better*. Accomplishment is achieved willingly because he is not worried about who gets the credit. Most important, he fervently believes that "Progressiveness is looking forward intelligently, looking within critically, and *working* on incessantly".

Knowledge of the Martial Arts also requires work. It, too, to use a phrase, is built by *bricks of habit.* Each new day of study adds another brick. Therefore, your Martial Arts future depends upon the habits you acquire. Acquire good habits and you will be able to build a firm foundation of BASICS. *An important reminder* -- as you spend time practicing, spend it well. Learn to discern what is or isn't practical. Constantly use logic and sound reasoning as guides of discernment. Remember, "Whatever you long for, yearn for, struggle for and hold persistently in your mind, you tend to become".

As you endeavor to research the Martial Arts, learn to develop tenancity and purpose. Do not apply only truths which you have discovered, but others that are meritoriously promising. Delve into the intricacies of the Art. Discover what further depths of sophistication lie within. Each new experience, each new development helps to build *self-confidence.* Once filled with *self-confidence* adhere to the following:"Self-confidence deserves to be carefully guarded because it is often the difference between success and failure". When you are armed with self-confidence seek even further avenues. Be creative. Creativity is not wrong if you stick to logic and sound reasoning. A comprehensive understanding of principles and how to properly apply them is another prerequisite when you are attempting to be creative. Creativity leads to higher learning, higher plateaus of experimentation, and the realization of how little you really know.

CHAPTER 2
DIVISION OF THE BASICS

To repeat what was stated in Volume II, BASICS are divided into five major divisions -- STANCES, MANEUVERS, BLOCKS, STRIKES, AND SPECIALIZED MOVES AND METHODS (these moves and methods are unrelated to the first four divisions that have distinct characteristics of their own). When BASICS from each division are employed, they may be used independently within their division, combined with those of another division, or combined with BASICS from all divisions.

The name for each BASIC move is often developed from three sources --method of execution, a specific part of the anatomy used in the execution, or the final position after execution. For example, if a BLOCK is delivered outside of your body structure and then *in* and toward it, it is considered an INWARD BLOCK (final position after execution). If the BLOCK is delivered inside of your body structure and then *out* and away from it, it is considered an OUTWARD BLOCK. If it is delivered *up* and above your body structure, it is considered an UPWARD BLOCK, and if it is executed *down* and below, a DOWNWARD BLOCK. A KNIFE-EDGE CHOP would be a descriptive term used for a specific part of the hand (anatomy) used in executing the CHOP. In using a STANCE, the final position taken may resemble a rider on a horse -- thus the term "HORSE STANCE" is given to this STANCE.

Direction is the fourth source used to name a BASIC move. As another example when you are using the descriptive term FRONT BALL KICK --*front* indicates the direction, *ball* that part of the anatomy you are to employ and *kick* the specific method you are to use when striking. SIDE THRUST KNIFE-EDGE KICK is self explanatory -- the term *side* tells you the direction, *thrust* the specific method of execution, *knife-edge* that portion of the anatomy used, *kick* that it is a method of striking employing the foot.

Each BASIC division is further divided into subdivisions. Please refer to the Chapters (in Volumes II and III) corresponding to each

3

of the five major divisions for a more detailed explanation.

As already emphasized in Volume II, it can be said that of the first four major divisions of BASICS, STANCES are literally postures of defense and offense, MANEUVERS are *methods of travel, and/or body positioning* to enhance defense or offense. BLOCKS are *methods of defense*, and STRIKES are *methods of offense*. The fifth division identifies those moves and methods that cannot be categorized under the first four divisions and that unquestionably contain individual characteristics of their own. SPECIALIZED MOVES AND METHODS can be used defensively as well as offensively.

Please thoroughly review the *charts* throughout this volume. Studying them (as well as those illustrated in Volume II) will give you a more comprehensive knowledge of the anatomical breakdown of the BASICS of the Martial Arts and how they relate to one another. These charts exclusively highlight practical methods and combinations. You are encouraged to experiment with these methods and combinations and cautioned not to loose sight of logic, sound reasoning and the proper use of principles.

ORGANIZATIONAL CHART ON BASICS

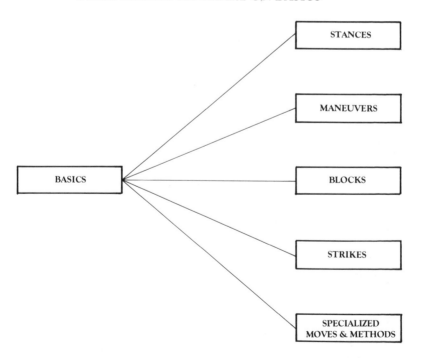

CHAPTER 3
BLOCKS

BLOCKS are primarily *defensive moves* employing physical contact to check, cushion, deflect, redirect, or stop an offensive move. On other occasions, it can be an anticipated *defensive position,* which, if correctly planned, can trigger a **BLOCK**. In the first case, physical effort was needed to counter your opponent's action. A third method which can be employed is to initiate a **BLOCK** on an opponent who is motionless at the time of your action. In this situation, a **BLOCK** is built into your offense so that your single action provides both a defense and offense. A fourth method involves *body checks* where pressure is placed on some part of the opponent's anatomy to restrain or prevent him from taking action. Although there may be no noticeable action from either party after pressure is applied, a **BLOCK**, nevertheless, can be rendered.

When executing a **BLOCK**, *physical contact* can occur: (1) when force meets force, (2) when force goes with force, (3) when force meets a neutral force, or (4) when a neutral force meets a neutral force. Because of these methods of *contact,* **BLOCKS** need to be defined. When *contact* is made in case #1, it is called a *STRIKING* **BLOCK** (a term used to describe this particular **BLOCK**. It does not necessarily inflict pain.) In case #2 a *PARRYING* **BLOCK**, in case #3 a *POSITIONED* **BLOCK** (or *CHECK*) (if you are motionless) or a *BLOCKING* **STRIKE** (if you initiate the action). (Another term used to describe this type of **BLOCK**. It too, does not necessarily inflict pain.) In case #4, it would be referred to as a *PINNING* **BLOCK** (or *CHECK*). The term *CHECK* is used in cases #3 and #4 because both are methods employed in *anticipation of* your opponent's *efforts.* In other words, these two types of **BLOCKS** aid in *CHECKING* your opponent's anticipated moves. Although both can be categorized as subdivisions of a *CHECK,* they, nevertheless, differ enough to merit their own identity.

In analyzing the various *types* of **BLOCKS**, it can be said that **BLOCKS** can be distinguished by the *methods* used *executing them.* Equally important, is the *anatomical positioning* necessary to anticipate your opponent's *execution methods.* An *INWARD* **BLOCK** and *INWARD PARRY* both use the descriptive term *INWARD.* However, it is the *method of execution* that alters their application; thus making them different.

You will discover as you progress that **STRIKES**, along with **BLOCKS**, share similar, as well as identical, *methods of execution.* In many instances, identical parts of the anatomy are used by both. The difference is determined by the *force* that is produced. For example, if your intended **BLOCK** rendered pain in addition to deflecting a punch or kick, it would then be considered a **STRIKE**. **BLOCKS** are intended to alter the direction of an attack or prevent action from taking off in another direction, but yet not render pain. **STRIKES** are intended to create pain or injury.

Another method that is identical in both **BLOCKS** and **STRIKES** is the manner in which they are *executed.* Delivery is at first relaxed, and then tenses at the point of contact and immediately relaxes again. The difference rests in the amount of *force* rendered.

It must be remembered that the *method of execution* is the manner in which a move, whether it is a defensive **BLOCK** or offensive **STRIKE**, is executed to produce maximum results. It involves the *type of Natural Weapon* used (clenched or open hand, finger pokes or claws, parts of the foot, etc.), the *force* produced, the *timing* (this factor determines *speed*), the *target chosen,* the *effect* intended (momentary paralysis, blindness, a fracture, etc.), and the *angle* or *path* (linear or circular) followed.

Although there may be exceptions to some of the above statements, as well as overlapping principles (depending upon either your or your opponent's viewpoint), what has been stated should suffice in the clarification of what principles and concepts are detailed in **BLOCKING**.

While most **BLOCKS** are executed with the *arms,* the *legs* should be restricted to the more adept since they require greater balance (using only one leg for weight support) timing, accuracy, flexibility (especially during the time of its execution and recovery), and controlled force (a rare ingredient that comes with experience).

What are some of the predicaments in which *LEG* **BLOCKS** would be effective? The answer -- situations where your arms are pinned or locked by a second opponent, and the possibility of the arms being tied or handcuffed. I do not mean to imply that the legs cannot be used as **BLOCKS** in other circumstances. However, one must always apply practical methods first before resorting to using unusual or less experienced movements. We should never be caught up in what looks good, but what would be practical at the time. Naturally, consideration must be given to the restrictions placed upon us.

ORGANIZATIONAL CHART ON BLOCKS

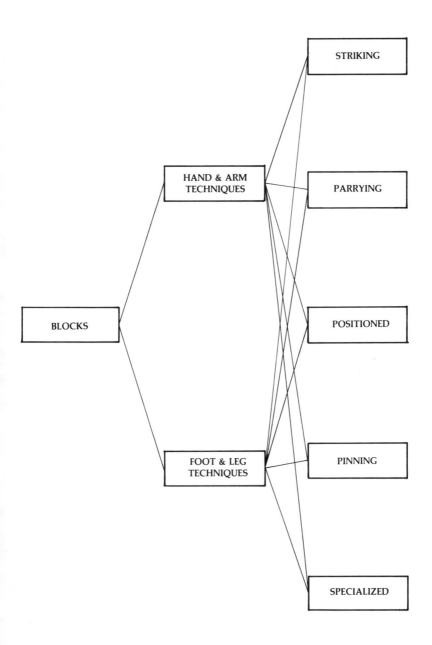

BASIC BLOCKS

There are many approaches and concepts which can be used to teach **BASIC BLOCKS** and *STRIKES*. It is my intention to commence from a **HORSE STANCE** with the hands cocked at the waist for **BLOCKS** utilizing **STRIKING** and **PARRYING**. This simplified procedure momentarily eliminates the co-ordination of footwork with arm movements. However, **BLOCKS** (using **STRIKING** and **PARRYING** methods) will be coordinated with **STANCE** changes in later volumes.

It is important that you learn to mentally visualize the direction of a supposed attack when you apply your **BASIC STRIKING** and **PARRYING** type **BLOCKS**. To aid you, geometric figures and other symbols will be superimposed periodically on the instructional photos. Through this means of monitoring, you can quickly acquaint yourself with directional angles necessary to maximize your efforts.

Initially, it is best to practice each **BLOCK** (using **STRIKING** and **PARRYING** methods) from a **HORSE STANCE** using only one arm at a time. That is, one arm **BLOCKS** and returns to the cocked position at the waist before another **BLOCK** is attempted. As you progress, co-ordinate both arms so that one arm is returning while the other is **BLOCKING**. Through diligent practice, it will become apparent that the movement of your **BLOCKING** arm, as it returns, may also be used as a **BLOCK**. See pages 120 to 123.

Regardless of the method used, practice each **BLOCK** slowly and relaxed in order to achieve proper form and continuity. Dynamic tension may be applied later to develop strength. Begin your **BLOCKS** with a relaxed arm -- tensing only at the time of contact. Premature tensing constipates your action; it literally puts *brakes* on your move before you reach your target. It is the *target* alone that should stop or *brake* your action. At the moment of contact, your **BLOCKING** arm should be rigid and tense. Relaxation must instantly reoccur so that the arm is available for further action whether it is to be used offensively or defensively.

Never overextend any of your **BLOCKS**. Restrict them to your *Zone of Protection* (see Volume IV Chapter Six). Precise arm extensions make them available for defense or offense. It is similar to playing a game of billiards where the "Q" ball not only sinks the designated ball into the pocket, but is positioned for the next shot. Availability as well as accessibility are important. Keep this in mind throughout the duration of your study.

I-1   There are valuable principles used in the game of billiards.

For purposes of exercise and exercise only, the opposite arm to the **BLOCKING** arm (for all **STRIKING** and **PARRYING** methods) will be simultaneously coordinated to render additional force. That is, added **BLOCKING** force is gained when the returning arm is forcefully retracted to match the effort of the **BLOCKING** arm. However, as you progress, this step will be eliminated since it does not take defense into consideration. Coordination with the lower body will be utilized instead. Thus, increased power will accompany your **BLOCKS** along with defensive hand positions.

It should be understood that although the **BLOCKS** (using **STRIKING** and **PARRYING** methods) presented here are defensive, they are also capable of becoming offensive. With extension and added force, they can instantly inflict pain or damage. When this occurs, a **BLOCK** then becomes a **STRIKE**. As you will notice, the **BLOCKS** are purposely cocked and then executed. This is a method of phonetically learning your **BLOCKS**. Although time consuming, it teaches you proper form. In time, the movements are shortened, the speed enhanced, and thus made more practical.

It is necessary at this point to explain some of the terms that will be used to describe **BLOCKS** (using **STRIKING AND** *PARRYING* methods). *INSIDE* refers to a **BLOCK** coming *in* and *toward* you. *OUTSIDE* is a **BLOCK** going from *inside out*. Therefore, no matter whether a punch or kick is delivered, a *RIGHT INWARD BLOCK* can strike on the *outside* or *inside* of an opponent's arm or leg. In other words, it is the direction in which the *BLOCKING* arm travels that determines whether a *BLOCK* is labeled *inward* or *outward*. The terms *upward* and *downward* are just what they imply.

ORGANIZATIONAL CHART ON STRIKING BLOCKS
(HAND & ARM)

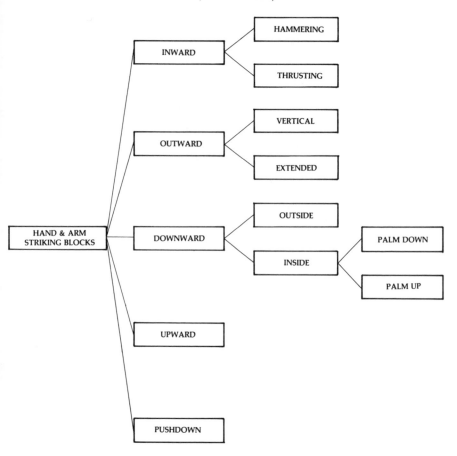

STRIKING **BLOCKS**

INWARD **BLOCK** -- This **BLOCK** is so labeled because in its execution, the arm moves *inside* or *toward* the front of the body. It is designed to counter *force with force* and redirect attempted punches or kicks to the head or chest. Such action results in a punch or kick being guided pass the left or right of your body and out of critical range.

The *INWARD* **BLOCK** is a *STRIKING* **BLOCK** (where the force of the **BLOCK** meets the force of the attack) and is of two varieties --*HAMMERING* and *THRUSTING*. *HAMMERING INWARD*

BLOCKS are highly recommended for the beginner since it teaches a beginner how to derive power from an *indirect* and *ideal* position. *THRUSTING INWARD* **BLOCKS** are for the more advanced students who learn that power can be obtained from a *direct* source. Learn both methods well. You never know when either can be useful. Circumstances often dictate a choice.

The visual approach using an imaginary square (box) superimposed over the photo should aid you in properly placing your hands and establishing the correct direction for your movements. The size of the square (box) is proportionate to the width of your shoulders. That is, each line forming the square (box) is the same length as the width of your shoulders. Refer to the illustrated photos for further instruction.

Note: Please note that the size of the superimposed square in the above photos are proportionate to the width of the shoulders.

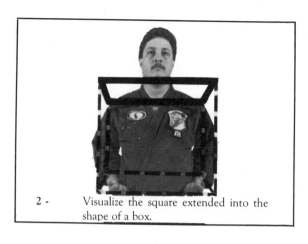

2 -   Visualize the square extended into the
shape of a box.

A *HAMMERING INWARD* **BLOCK** is so called because the method of execution greatly resembles the motion used in pounding a hammer. Although this **BLOCK** is one continuous motion, it will be helpful to learn the *HAMMERING INWARD* in steps. From the starting position (hands cocked at the waist) (photos 1a thru 2), raise your right clenched fist and rotate it counterclockwise to cocking position two (photos 3a thru 3c). At this point, the right fist is at the back of your upper right corner (closest to your right shoulder) of the imaginary square with your right forearm pressing against the bicep and your palm facing out. On your next move, your right arm travels diagonally from your right shoulder to the forward left corner of your imaginary square (box) (photos 3a thru 3c). As this move is executed, the forearm leaves the bicep and your hand rotates clockwise so that the hammer portion of your right fist ends the motion (like a hammer pounding a nail). Both the elbow and the fist move in the same direction to the target. Viewing this move from the front, you will find that the elbow rests at the center of the body (opposite the solar plexus) and the fist in front of the opposite (left) shoulder. It is important not to extend the arm beyond this point and to have your right elbow anchored. This increases your defensive cover; thus allowing you greater margin for error. Please note that the right wrist is straight.

To complete the cycle, place your right arm in a cocked position at your waist. Repeat the process using your left arm. Practice using one arm at a time and then coordinate both so that as one **BLOCKS,** the other cocks, etc.

Although it is recommended that your action stops at the forward left corner of your imaginary square (box), this is only used as a point of reference. The *depth, height* and *width* of your **BLOCK** can be altered as long as you avoid extremes.

12

| FRONT VIEW | SIDE VIEW | TOP VIEW |

AN IMPORTANT SUGGESTION

Make sure that your thumb is tucked in while executing inward blocks. A loose thumb can be sprained or broken. Hitting a weapon incorrectly or catching your thumb in clothing can cause this to happen. Why allow mistakes to happen when they can easily be avoided?

4a

b

c

NOTE: The importance of anchoring the elbows cannot be overemphasized. It gives you greater protection because it allows you margin for error. Equally important is the fact that it adds power to the force of your block.

HELPFUL HINT

As a helpful suggestion, place a knife in your right hand as you practice your *HAMMERING INWARD* **BLOCK**. Cocking your hand to your shoulder, rotate your fist so that the blade of the knife is away from you. In executing the **BLOCK**, rotate your fist in a clockwise direction and stab the forward corner of your imaginary square with the point of your blade. If the forward left corner of your imaginary square was wood, the position of your right fist would have to be angled correctly for the blade to stick in the wood effectively; thus, the necessity of correctly positioning your hand.

AN ADDITIONAL SUGGESTION

I suggest that you use the stronger, faster, and most coordinated of your arms to block with in actual combat. Predetermined labeling requires too much time to think of a matching counter. You cannot afford to jeopardize your reaction time. Therefore, whether your opponent utilizes his right or left arm, you should use your most coordinated arm. Try it; you'll find it works.

THRUSTING INWARD **BLOCK** -- involves direct action. There is no prolonged path to follow, no cocking; no need to pronounce your move phonetically. Power is derived instantly. Only while practicing will you be requested to start your **BLOCK** with your hands cocked at the waist. In a real crisis, you are to start your action from the position your hand is in at the time. Even with the hands cocked at the waist, the motion is direct and is to be executed as a *thrust.* As the fist (palm up) leaves its cocked position, it makes a quarter turn (counterclockwise) as it shoots from the lower right back corner of your imaginary box to the upper left hand corner of the box. Like the *HAMMERING INWARD* **BLOCK**, the *hammer portion* of the fist makes contact as the action ends. At this point, a *HAMMERING* and *THRUSTING INWARD* **BLOCK** are identical in appearance and, if properly executed, equal in force. Place the hand in a cocked position and execute a left *THRUSTING INWARD* **BLOCK**. After practicing the **BLOCKS** one at a time, coordinate both so that as one **BLOCKS** the other cocks, etc.

16

Visualize a hinge on this corner.

7 -   When dropping back with your left foot from a Training Horse Stance into a Right Neutral Bow Stance your imaginary square should be visualized as stationary. It does not move with the angle change of your body. In fact, the right rear corner of your imaginary square should be thought of as having a free swinging hinge.

OUTWARD **BLOCKS** are **BLOCKS** that are delivered from *inside out*. That is, they travel from the *inside* framework of your body to a point *out* and *away* from it. They produce the reverse effect of an *INWARD* **BLOCK**. These *BLOCKS* are also designed to counter force with force and to redirect attempted punches or kicks to the head or chest. Like an *INWARD*, an *OUTWARD* **BLOCK** can direct a punch, or kick so that it is guided pass the left or right of your body and out of critical range.

There are two types of *OUTWARD* **BLOCKS** -- *VERTICAL* and *EXTENDED*. The *EXTENDED OUTWARD* is the stronger of the two as well as the most useful. It uses the strongest portion of the forearm -- hence is better suited to withstand force. In addition to its strength, it is used for *long range encounters*. The *VERTICAL OUTWARD* is basically for *close range attacks*. It can be used for close **BLOCKS**, *CHECKS*, or as the second part of a *DOUBLE* **BLOCK**. Both are not to extend beyond the *zone of protection* (see Volume   IV   Chapter Six).   Note that *OUTWARDS* and *INWARDS* accomplish the same purposes.

The *VERTICAL OUTWARD* is given this name because of the position the forearm is in at the time of delivery. It is used primarily as a defense for close range encounters. From the start (with your hands cocked to the waist), have your right fist move horizontally (palm up) to the bottom left

17

rear corner of your imaginary square (photos 8c and d). As your right fist reaches this corner, immediately turn your right palm down. Without stopping, have your right fist go midway to the upper left side of your imaginary box (photo 9a). When your right fist reaches this point, turn your right fist so that your right palm faces you and continue your motion to the midpoint of the upper right side of your imaginary square (photos 9b and c). Your right arm should not extend beyond this point. Make sure that your right forearm is vertical and that your right fist and elbow are in line with one another. Using explosive torque and with your right elbow anchored, you should be able to exert maximum power and protection. Protecting as large an area as possible allows you a greater margin for error. As is true of all *BLOCKS*, the *depth, height* and *width* of your *VERTICAL OUTWARD* can be altered as long as extreme movements are avoided.

8 - Again visualize a complete box that extends from your shoulder to your waist.

Note: To redirect or deviate the course of your opponent's strikes does not mean to guide them to another vulnerable area. You are to guide them away from your body.

ANALYTICAL STUDY OF A *VERTICAL OUTWARD*

The *EXTENDED OUTWARD* gets its name because it extends farther than the *VERTICAL OUTWARD*. From the start (with your hands cocked at the waist), the arm moves horizontally (palm up) to the left rear bottom corner of your imaginary square (photos 11a and 11b). Without stopping, have your right fist proceed diagonally to the upper right hand corner of your imaginary square (photos 11c and 11d), torquing your right fist counterclockwise so that the palm of your right hand is away from you. As you will notice, it is the *hammer portion* of your fist that makes contact, extending farther from the body than the *VERTICAL OUTWARD*. Although the right forearm is at a slight angle, the elbow is, nevertheless, anchored so that protection is maximized and error compensated for. When practicing, *do not* extend your fist beyond the point indicated. Under more realistic conditions, you may alter your *height, width* and *depth* and confine your move within the area of your *protection zone*. From the direction your palms are facing, it should be evident that the two *OUTWARD BLOCKS* use opposite sides of the forearm.

11a

b   c   d

12a

b

c

DOWNWARD BLOCKS are BLOCKS that are delivered, using the motion of a pendulum below the waist. They can swing *in* or *out* to protect the lower half of the body against grabs, punches, kicks, etc. Countering *force with force,* they can guide an attack pass the left or right of your body, thus eliminating the chance of contact.

DOWNWARD BLOCKS are of two varieties -- OUTSIDE and INSIDE. The OUTSIDE DOWNWARD is the stronger, as well as most useful of the two. The OUTWARD motion is better suited to withstand force. The choice is determined mainly by the angle of the attack and the position your body is in at the time of the attack. Both are to be confined within your *zone of protection.* See Volume IV.

The INSIDE DOWNWARD consists of two varieties -- PALMDOWN and PALM UP. The INSIDE DOWNWARD PALM DOWN version has greater reach while the other is somewhat restricted because of the muscle tension that is involved.

The OUTSIDE DOWNWARD is executed by bringing your right forearm across your waist horizontally with the palm of your right fist facing up. Complete your first move by having your right fist reach the midpoint of the left side of your imaginary square* (photos 13a thru 13c   ).   While reaching this point, do not have your upper body lean forward. This movement should aid you in increasing the power of your BLOCK, as well as the area of protection.

The next move is the BLOCK itself. Have your right clenched fist, palm up, rotate counterclockwise so that the hammer portion of your right fist leads your right forearm as it travels *down* and *out* in an arc to the final position (photos 13b thru 13e   ).   Your right arm should stop mid-way on the right side of your imaginary square. Have your right fist line up above and in front of your right knee with your right arm slightly bent to protect the elbow.

Have your right arm return to the starting position (hands cocked at the waist) by retracing the path of delivery. Coordinating both arms, one *blocks* as the other returns, have your *blocking* arm travel above the arm that is returning.

*NOTE: Please note that your imaginary square is located at HIP level. In this case, the size of your imaginary square is determined by the width of your hips and not your shoulders.

13a

b

c

d

e

ANALYTICAL STUDY OF AN *OUTSIDE DOWNWARD*

14a

b

c

    INSIDE DOWNWARD, PALM DOWN and *PALM UP,* are used to redirect or stop a low *STRIKE.* They serve the same purpose as the *OUTSIDE DOWNWARD* except that the movement is in the opposite direction. That is, the arm travels below the waist from *outside - in.* As previously stated, the *PALM DOWN* has more reach, but the *PALM UP version is stronger.*

24

INSIDE DOWNWARD, **PALM DOWN** -- With your hands cocked at the waist, your right arm loops *out* and to your right with the palm facing you. Complete the loop by redirecting your action *in* and *toward* you (photos 15a and 15b). As your right arm travels in (palm down), have it move from the midpoint on the right side of your imaginary square (at hip level) to the midpoint of the left side of your imaginary square (photos 15c and 15d). The right arm is almost stiff at this point, swinging from the shoulder (without leaning) to the final position. The inner forearm is used to *BLOCK*. Cock your right hand back to the right side of your waist and follow through with your left arm.

15a

b

c

d

ANALYTICAL STUDY OF AN *INSIDE DOWNWARD —*
PALM DOWN

INSIDE DOWNARD, **PALM UP** -- With your hands cocked at the waist, your right arm loops *out* and to your right as your right palm turns *out* and *away* from you. Complete the loop by redirecting your action *in* and *toward* you (photos 17a and 17b). As your right arm moves *in,* rotate your right fist clockwise (palm up) and have the hammer portion of your fist move from midpoint on the right side of your imaginary square (at hip level) to the halfway point, dead center, of your imaginary square (photos 17c and 17d). Your right forearm also rotates with the fist, but it is the hammer portion of the fist that leads the action to the point of contact. Notice in photo 17d that the hand does not come pass the center of your body. In photo 17d the right arm is slightly bent at a definite angle, yet the fist is low. When returning, the right hand is pulled to the waist before continuing the action with your left arm.

A special note regarding both types of *INSIDE DOWNWARDS.* In coordinating both arms, using one to block with as the other returns, the arms do not crossover each other as they do in executing the *OUTSIDE DOWNWARD.*

TOP VIEW

FRONT VIEW

ANALYTICAL STUDY OF AN *INSIDE DOWNWARD* — PALM UP

An *UPWARD BLOCK* is primarily a defense against overhead attacks. It is a ricochetting *BLOCK* that does not resist the entire momentum of the attack. The forearm rises, makes contact, and immediately assumes a diagonal position which causes the attack to be deflected and directed to the side.

The UPWARD BLOCK is really one smooth continuous movement. However, to simplify learning, it will be divided into two parts. The first half of the move resembles an uppercut punch and provides most of the power that goes into the second half snap. As an aid, we will use a 2' x 3' board or cardboard in addition to superimposing an imaginary box to the photo. Hang the board or cardboard in front of you, and midway between your body (photos 19 and 20). Place the top of the board on a level with your eyebrows photo 20).   From waist level, have your right clenched fist (palm up) travel to the lower portion of the board (photo 21a). Have your fist and elbow slide up along the right side of the board (palm toward you). The elbow must also follow up the center so that as it is seen from the front, the forearm is vertical (photo 21b). The use of the board will compel you to travel in an upward path that is dead center with your body. The first step ends (not the motion) as your right fist reaches eyebrow level (photo 21c). During the last half of your move, rotate your right fist vigorously counterclockwise (the palm turned out and away from you) and direct it diagonally to the outer left hand corner of your imaginary square. Your right arm torques up and to your left, on a gradual incline and ends in the final position (photo 21d). Closely examine the angle and position of your right forearm. You will notice the UPWARD BLOCK is roughly centered above and in front of your body. Your right wrist should remain straight throughout the entire maneuver.

Returning to your original position, have your right arm retrace the same path after delivery. Execute a left UPWARD BLOCK. When both arms are coordinated to work consecutively, the arm that is BLOCKNG should cross in front of the arm that is returning.

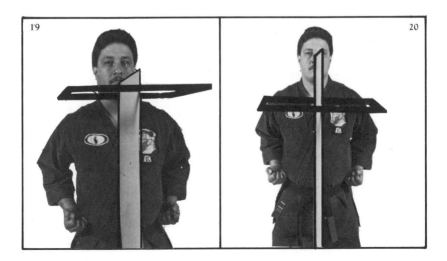

19   20

ANALYTICAL STUDY OF AN *UPWARD BLOCK*

23a   a

NOTE: Although both points of view are different they are nevertheless the same type of block. This is true of all blocks under the title of *ANALYTICAL STUDY OF.*

A *PUSHDOWN BLOCK* occurs more frequently with modifications of the *BASIC* movement. It primarily uses the angle of the forearm (as seen in photo 24d) to deflect *STRIKES* to the lower regions of the body. The heel of the palm may also be used as a *BLOCK, CHECK,* or weapon. It is not a common **BLOCK,** but, nevertheless, warrants your attention and consideration. Don't fail to add it to your alphabets of motion.

With your right fist cocked at your waist, begin by opening your right hand and raising it, palm up, until the right forearm is resting against the bicep (photo 24b). Have your right hand move diagonally downward until it is at the center of your body (photo 24c). A common mistake is to raise the elbow. Direct the elbow *forward* and *down.* At the exact moment the move is completed and in anticipation of resistance, tense your entire right arm. To complete the cycle, your right hand returns to the right side of your waist as your fist closes. The entire sequence is done very smoothly. Repeat the same movement using your left arm.

NOTE: The above photos demonstrate two points of view -- top and front. The "a" photo at the top matches the "a" photo at the bottom. This is true of "b" through "d". It is hoped that these photos aid you in properly executing this particular block.

25a

b

c

AN EDUCATIONAL REVIEW

If your arm was traveling clockwise or counterclockwise, it would only appear to be traveling in a 360° circle. Yet, innocent as these circles may seem, they contain a number of surprising answers. Within each of the circular moves (both clockwise and counterclockwise), are many of the blocks previously detailed. A stop-action camera would quickly reveal variations of an inward, outward, upward, and downward block. In short, each of these blocks are no more than stop-action segments of a 360° circle. Please refer to the following illustrations for further elaboration.

a   b

NOTE: The above photos demonstrate some of the blocks that can stem out of a circular movement when (a) traveling counterclockwise or (b) clockwise (from demonstrator's point of view). Please take note in (a) of your *Inward Block*, flowing to a *Downward Block* and up into an *Upward Block*. In (b) the arm starts as an *Inside Downward* (palm down) as it then transposes into a *Vertical Outward*, *Extended Outward*, and back down into an *Inside Downward Block* (palm up).

ORGANIZATIONAL CHART ON PARRYING BLOCKS
(HAND & ARM)

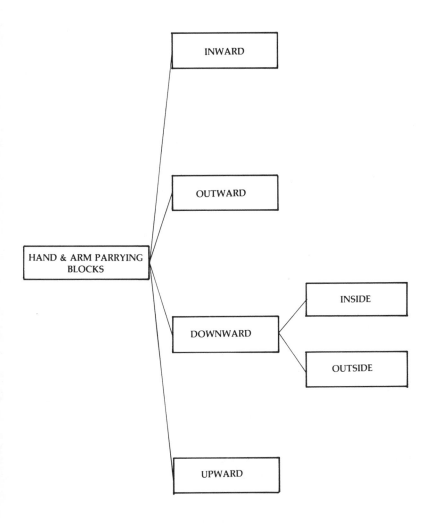

PARRYING BLOCKS

INWARD PARRY -- This **BLOCK** is designed to go *with force* and redirect attempted **STRIKES** to the head or chest. Like the *STRIKING* **BLOCKS**, this action can result in a **STRIKE** being guided pass the left or right of your body and out of critical range.

Picture an imaginary square at shoulder level. Mentally draw a triangle inside of your imaginary square (photos 26a thru 26c). With your hands cocked at your waist, your right hand comes up to a point on your imaginary triangle (the front midpoint of your imaginary square) as you open your right hand (fingers extended and joined). See photo 26b . From this point (your motion has not stopped), move your right hand from front to rear as well as right to left to the left rear corner of your imaginary square (photo 26c). Face your right palm out and to your left during the completion of your movement.

Cock your right hand to the right side of your waist and commence a left *INWARD PARRY.*

ANALYTICAL STUDY OF AN *INWARD PARRY*

27a

b

c

OUTWARD PARRY -- This **BLOCK** is also designed to serve the same purposes as an *INWARD PARRY*. The difference lies in the angle and direction of execution.

With your hands cocked at your waist, your right hand comes up to the point of your imaginary triangle (front midpoint of your imaginary square) as you open your right hand (fingers extended and joined). See photo 28a . From this point (your motion has not stopped), move your right hand from front to rear, but this time from left to right to the right rear corner of your imaginary square (photo 28b). Use the back of your open hand to parry and redirect the **STRIKES** to your head or chest.

Cock your right hand to the right side of your waist and commence a left *OUTWARD PARRY*.

ANALYTICAL STUDY OF AN *OUTWARD PARRY*

INSIDE DOWNWARD PARRY -- This **BLOCK** is for **STRIKES** delivered to vital areas below the waist. The **BLOCK** goes along with the force of the attack in an attempt to redirect its course.

Picture an imaginary square at hip level and add a triangle within the same square (photo 30a). With hands cocked at the waist, your right hand circles counterclockwise (hand is still clenched). Continue the movement to the top point of your imaginary triangle (photo 30b) and use the inside of your right palm (with fingers extended and joined) to go from the top point of your imaginary triangle to the left inner back corner of your imaginary square (photo 30c). The outer portion of the hand is used to *parry* the attack. Recock your right hand and execute a left *OUTSIDE DOWNWARD PARRY*.

31a

b

c

OUTSIDE DOWNWARD PARRY -- This is another method used to **BLOCK STRIKES** delivered to vital areas below the waist. The **BLOCK** goes along with the force of the attack in an attempt to redirect its course. This course is in the opposite direction of an *INSIDE DOWNWARD PARRY*.

Picture an imaginary square at the level of your hip and superimpose an imaginary triangle inside of the square (photo 32a). With both hands cocked at your waist have your right hand circle counterclockwise (hand is still clenched). Continue the motion of your right hand to the top point of your imaginary triangle (photo 32a), open your hand (with fingers extended and joined) and move your hand from the top point of your imaginary triangle to the right inner back corner of your imaginary square (photo 32b). The outer portion of the hand is used to *parry* the attack. Recock your right hand and execute a left *OUTSIDE DOWNWARD PARRY.*

33a

b

c

UPWARD PARRY -- This **BLOCKING** method is used for **STRIKES** delivered to the head. It is of great assistance in *PARRYING* **STRIKES** over and above your head by riding the force of your opponent's action.

It resembles an *UPWARD* **BLOCK** with two exceptions. During the last phase of the move, the hand opens, *palm up,* and the arm circles over, back, and toward you (photos 34d and 34e).

Like the *UPWARD* **BLOCK**, the *UPWARD PARRY* is really one smooth continuous movement. For purposes of clarity, it, too, should be divided into two parts. The first half of the move is identical to an uppercut punch and provides the build-up power for the snap involved in the last half of your action. From waist level, have your right clenched fist (palm up) **STRIKE** vertically to the middle of your body in an uppercut fashion (photo 34b). When your right fist reaches eyebrow level, start the last half of your motion by vigorously rotating your right fist counterclockwise (having your right hand open with your right palm facing upward) and direct your right arm over, back, and toward you in a circular orbit (photo 34e). Closely examine the angle and position of your forearm and be certain it proportionately frames your head.

Returning the *UPWARD PARRY* to its original position, have your right arm retrace its delivered path. Proceed with a left *UPWARD PARRY.* When alternating *UPWARD PARRIES,* have your **BLOCKING** arm cross in front of the arm that is returning.

34a

b

c

ANALYTICAL STUDY OF AN *UPWARD PARRY*

35a

b

c

36 - Example of the forearm being used to parry.

NOTE: Parrying blocks are not restricted to only using the hands. Other variations employing the forearm, elbow, etc. can also be utilized. Regardless, the method of execution remains the same. In short, other body parts using the same motions and paths can be substituted.

POSITIONED **BLOCKS**

Although these **BLOCKS** require the arms or legs to be placed in various height and depth positions, they are used to thwart the efforts of an opponent. Proper arm and leg positioning can cause an offensive move to be **BLOCKED** during delivery. Even though your opponent initiates the action, your statuette position can still cause a **BLOCK**. Such positions can be achieved by the correct placement of one arm, both arms, or both arms and a leg.

Depending upon the type of stance you assume, (whether one foot is back and the other forward), you would have a forward, rear arm, or both to position. If both arms are used, one should be high and the other low. They should not be at the same level at the same time. Your vital areas would, therefore, be exposed and vulnerable to attack.

The forward or rear arm can be placed in any one of four positions (with innovations) -- *INWARD, OUTWARD, UPWARD,* or *DOWNWARD.* These are the final positions your arms are in before executing the **STRIKING BLOCKS** -- the hands can be closed or open.

The following are combinations that can be used utilizing both arms from a *RIGHT NEUTRAL BOW STANCE.*

ORGANIZATIONAL CHART ON POSITIONED BLOCKS
(HAND & ARM)

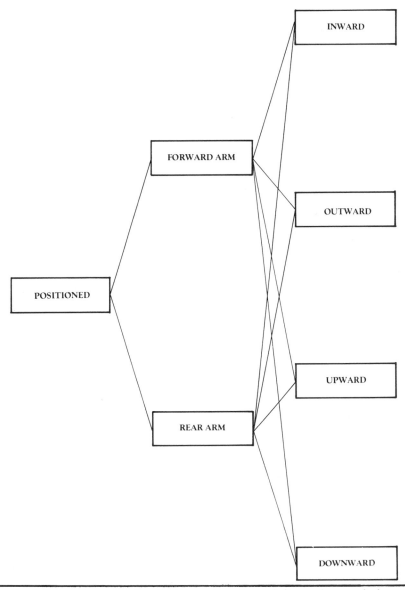

Special Note: Your arms or legs should be positioned at a safe distance from your body so that they may effectively absorb the shock of your opponent's strikes. It is also imperative that you position your arms or legs close enough to your body so that you minimize your target exposure.

In addition, be sure to have your arms, legs or combinations of both form wedges during periods of transition from one position to another. This is another safeguard to protect and trap strikes as they occur.

Forward arm - right outward
Rear arm - left inside downward
(palm down)

Forward arm - right downward
Rear arm - left inward
(Hands can be open)

Forward arm - right inward
Rear arm - left downward
(Hands can be open)

Forward arm - right inside downward
(palm down)
Rear arm - left outward

Forward arm - right upward
Rear arm - left pushdown

Forward arm - right pushdown
Rear arm - left upward

Position Block including arms and leg
(From a left one-leg stance)

Forward arm - right inward
Rear arm - left downward
Forward leg - raise knee

These positions are some of the possible combinations. Use your imagination to discover other variables. However, remember to alternate hands.

PINNING BLOCKS

As previously stated, *PINNING* **BLOCKS** are methods employing *body checks* to restrain or prevent an opponent from activating moves which he would have hoped to use as counters. It requires the *POSITIONING* of your arms, legs, or body *against* various parts of your opponent's anatomy to prevent anticipated moves. These *contact placements* can be done prior to, during, or after an attack regardless of who initiates the attack. The type of *PINNING* **BLOCK** applied would depend upon your or your opponent's stance position, range, or posture at the time of the encounter. A single *contact placement* could be used to prevent your opponent from taking further action. In some instances, several *contact placements* may be required to do the job.

Although these *PINNING* **BLOCKS** are necessary to prevent your opponent from taking action (for the moment), it should in no way hamper your efforts in quickly countering your opponent. If your efforts are hampered, as those of your opponent's, then by all means revise your training methods.

This principle of *checking* is not commonly used by advocates of the Martial Arts and, therefore, should be more readily adopted. Make every effort to condition yourself to apply this principle. It is a principle that not only prevents anticipated action, but unintentional action that might accidently cause your defeat. The very fact that intentional as well as unintentional moves are prevented from happening makes the principle worth incorporating.

There are two types of *PINNING* **BLOCKS** -- *PUSHING* and *VICE-LIKE*.

PUSHING PINNING **BLOCKS** employ *pressing* or *nudging* contact methods to immobilize an opponent. When applied, it nullifies the use of *natural weapons* because it controls the leverage of an opponent. As a result, these *PUSHING* methods can cause an opponent's arms to be *PINNED* to his own body, his body *PINNED* to a wall or other surrounding objects, one leg *pressed* against the other, his weight forced to the floor as well as the use of other methods that hamper leverage. The degree of force executed by a blow or kick is proportionate to the degree of its leverage capability. Restrict an opponent's leverage and you restrict his power. Deeper insights to leverage control will be further detailed when we discuss the control of *height, width,* and *depth zones.* (See Volume IV Chapter Six .)

The following are examples of *PUSHING PINNING* **BLOCKS**:

46 - Single Hand Pin.

47 - Double-Hand Pin.

48 - Pin against the wall.

49 - Pin against the floor.

VICE-LIKE PINNING **BLOCKS** employ immobilizing methods that control a part of your opponent's anatomy with yours. Other objects are not generally used in the process (can be in advanced training with weapons). *GRABBING* is a *vice-like pinning method* that can be coupled with a *PUSHING PIN*. **HUGGING** falls under this category. *PINCHING* your opponent's arm between your forearm and bicep is another *vice-like method* of employing a *PINNING* **BLOCK** ending in an *arm lock*. *Leg locks* using your leg to immobilize your opponent are still other *VICE-LIKE PINNING* **BLOCKS**. See the following examples for further clarification. (Refer to Chapter Five.)

50 - is an example of Grabbing.   51 - depicts Pinching with your forearm and bicep.   52 - demonstrates a method of Hugging.

53 - illustrates an Arm Lock.

54 - is an example of a Leg Lock.

ORGANIZATIONAL CHART ON PINNING BLOCKS
(HAND & ARM)

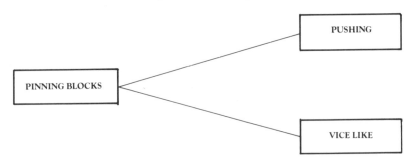

ORGANIZATIONAL CHART ON SPECIALIZED BLOCKS
(HAND & ARM)

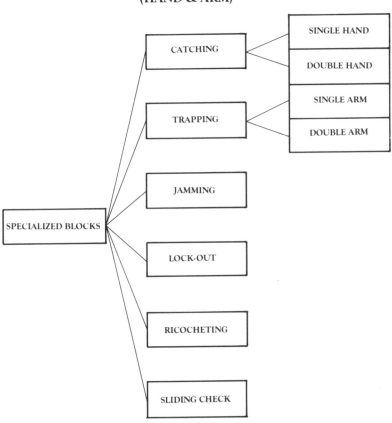

CATCHING and *TRAPPING* are *specialized methods* of **BLOCKING**. They are *special* because they require two or more methods of **BLOCKING** to complete the move. A single method of execution would not warrant this *special* category.

As you will discover, all **BASIC** categories employ *specialized methods;* however, their *specialties* result from their own distinguishable characteristics. Differences within the major categories will be detailed as well as clarified.

CATCHING resembles *GRABBING,* but is, nevertheless, technically different. *CATCHING* is intercepting a **STRIKE** *while it is in motion. GRABBING* occurs *after a CATCH* has been completed. In other words, **GRABBING** generally occurs *after an opponent's motion is brought under control. GRABS* often follow other methods of defense and are great aids in prolonging control. They are helpful *motion deterrents* .

CATCHING is just what it implies. It is intercepting, guiding, and capturing **STRIKES** already in flight. Precise timing is required, and therefore, it is not recommended for the beginner. Because it is used to redirect and/or stop a **STRIKE** from hitting you (although *special*), it is categorized as a **BLOCK**.

A *CATCH* employs two methods in its execution -- it *RIDES* the force of the **STRIKE** before *GRABBING* and controlling it. Technically then, a *CATCH* is a *PARRYING* method of **BLOCKING** since it *RIDES* the force and combines with a *GRAB*.

There are two types of *CATCHES -- SINGLE HAND* and *DOUBLE HAND.* The ways in which they can be applied are as follows:

a thru d - demonstrates a Single Hand Grab.

b

c

d

56a

55

a thru c - is an example of a Double Hand Grab. A Twist or Wrist Lock could be effectively employed before or after a kick has been executed.

TRAPPING is sometimes classified as just another variation of *CATCHING*. For a more precise definition *TRAPPING* is any stratagem designed to *CATCH* a *natural weapon* and preventing it from escaping. It, too, redirects, stops, and captures **STRIKES** *while in flight*. *GRABS* are the end result of a capture. The **STRIKE** is immobilized and brought under control. Close examination, however, will reveal several technical differences. *CATCHES* are primarily localized to one specific area of the opponent's body. *TRAPPING* involves divided areas of concentration; it normally requires the application of two arms to complete the move. However, under rare and *special* conditions, a single arm could be used. Even then, more than one specific area of the opponent's body is involved in its application. The single arm versions are again reserved for the more adept.

CATCHING with two hands requires that both hands concentrate on the *same* part of the opponent's anatomy, as they employ *identical* **BLOCKING** methods. When *TRAPPING*, each arm employs *contrasting* **BLOCKING** methods. For example, one arm may utilize a *PARRYING* **BLOCK** while the other simultaneously uses a **STRIKING BLOCK**. The similarity between the two (*CATCHING* and *TRAPPING*) lies with the *GRABBING* that concludes the action. *GRABBING*, as in *CATCHING* is the final step used to control an opponent after *TRAPPING* a **STRIKE**. In both instances, control is applied until a follow-up move is executed. Unless, of course, one hand controls as the other strikes; both hands control as the foot strikes or other combinations deemed practical at the time.

TRAPPING is divided into two categories -- *DOUBLE ARM* and *SINGLE ARM*. They are described as follows:

57a thru d - is a classic example of a Single Arm Trap. Once the arm is trapped, follow-up strikes can be effectively used. With proper planning, the trapped arm can be sprained or broken by the arm that is controlling it. The number of variables are endless. It is your knowledge of these variables along with your skill that determines your success or failure.

58 - illustrates a Double-Arm Trap. Follow-up strikes such as an elbow or knee can very easily end the fracus. Forcing an opponent to the wall prior to executing an elbow or knee strike can increase the sandwiching effect of your action. Takedowns can also be employed to force an opponent to the ground.

JAMMING is another *specialized method* of **BLOCKING**. It involves the delivery of a **STRIKE** to crowd or force an opponent's *natural weapon* back and against his joint to prevent it from moving or functioning. JAMMING can also be accomplished by forcing an opponent's limb against other parts of his anatomy. For example, after catching an opponent's arm, it can be shoved and **JAMMED** into his face. This act would doubtless render temporary or permanent disability. It is an effective method and should be included as part of your vocabulary of motion.

59a thru d - illustrates how both of your arms can be used to jam your opponent's arms.

Follow-up strikes, can be employed much more effectively when your opponent's weapons are jammed.

LOCK-OUT is a *specialized* **BLOCK** used to delay an opponent from counterattacking. The unusual feature about this **BLOCK** is that it originates from the tail end of an offensive **STRIKE**. Instead of retrieving the **STRIKE**, it is purposely **LOCKED-OUT** to occupy space, disturb balance, and disrupt timing. The result -- space is not available for an opponent to quickly reset himself or retaliate. Ideal posture is necessary to maximize force when counterattacking. The mere fact that this brief delay *checks* an opponent from counter attacking labels the *LOCK-OUT* a **BLOCK**.

Other methods may be applied after a *LOCK-OUT* to further disturb balance and disrupt timing. Pushes, grabs, and checks are a few examples. Mid-range *natural weapons* may be applied by the more adept or sophisticated *take-downs* by the highly skilled.

60 a thru d - is a good example of a Lock-Out Punch. Such action prevents an opponent from regaining a postural position that can effectively activate aggressive action.

RICOCHETING **BLOCK** is a **BLOCK** that is generally built into an aggressive **STRIKE**. It is the execution of a single move to accomplish two purposes -- defense and offense. It, therefore, can be compared with writing in *short hand* because it is a *short hand* method of motion.

A *RICOCHETING* **BLOCK** can be applied strictly as a defense, but is seldom used in this manner. A highly effective substitute would be to apply the **BLOCK** and immediately place the **BLOCKING** arm in a defensive position (**POSITION BLOCK**).

61a thru c is - a good example of "short-hand motion" where a defense and offense concurrently takes place during a "single action." As you will notice in **b**, a block takes place before the fist of the same arm and action strikes to your opponent's face.

SLIDING CHECK is a *specialized* **PINNING BLOCK**. *Pressing* or *nudging* contact methods to immobilize an opponent are also employed. However, these *checking* methods travel on an opponent's body by *sliding* from one leverage point to another. During the course of each *slide*, constant body contact is maintained so as not to allow for retaliation.

Usually one hand checks while the other strikes, but both can be used simultaneously. Choice and circumstances will determine this.

62 a - shows the right hand grabbing the right shoulder of your opponent. The left hand is cocked and ready for action.

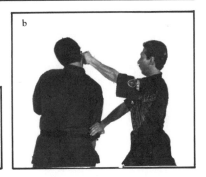

b - shows the right hand sliding down the right arm of your opponent (keeping that arm in constant check) while the left fist simultaneously strikes to your opponent's face.

It is extremely important that you learn to utilize blocks (detailed in this chapter) and strikes (detailed in the following chapter) from various positions that either you or your opponent may be found in during combat. (See chapters on TARGETS and ZONES in Volume IV.) As you will discover, some blocks and strikes are only effective from specific positions -- positions that you or your opponent may be in at the time they are executed. Knowledge of how to employ blocks and strikes while either you or your opponent are standing, kneeling, or are on his or your back or stomach can help to increase your chances of survival. DON'T FORGET -- the greater your knowledge of existing variables the more certain you are of victory. Therefore, as you view the vast number of blocks and strikes illustrated in this volume, contemplate reality. Realize that it is possible for you to be forcibly placed in a precarious position, or that you can do the same to your opponent. Naturally, once you have gained this knowledge, you can randomly choose specific positions that strategically give you the greater advantage while you are blocking or striking.

SPECIAL NOTE: Many of the blocks discussed can be converted into strikes as your proficiency increases. To go one step further, not only are defensive and offensive moves interchangeable, they become increasingly effective when the reverse motion of your moves are also included as part of your arsenal of beneficial variables.

This chapter would not be complete if your feet and legs were not included as essential methods that could be used for blocking. Having your arms tied, handcuffed or grabbed from the rear, especially where two opponents are involved, would force you to depend upon your feet and legs. Similar solutions utilizing the feet and legs would be necessary if you were thrown or forced to the ground on your back, or stomach. The following photos illustrate answers to some of the predicaments mentioned.

ORGANIZATIONAL CHART ON STRIKING BLOCKS
(FOOT & LEG)

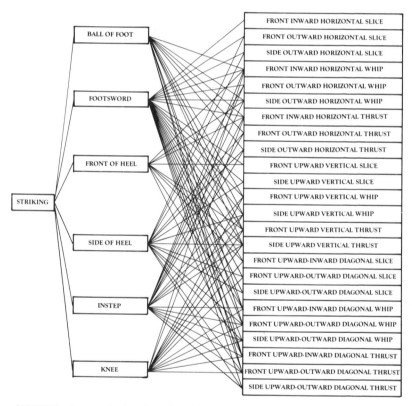

NOTE: The above methods are but a few of the more practicle variables that can be used. Other parts of the foot can be used, such as the back of the heel, against attacks from the flank or rear. Other combinations of the above can be utilized.

63a

b

c

d

The above sequence demonstrates the use of a Slicing Kick (Front Inward Horizontal Slice) to block the intended kick of an opponent.

The following sequence demonstrates the use of a Thrust Kick (Front Outward Hoizontal Thrust) to stop your opponent's kick before it can become a devastating weapon.

64a

b

c

As you will notice in the illustrated sequence, the hands can be used as an integral part in controlling your opponent. The use of continual checks are necesssary deterrants.

65a and b - demonstrates a "Side Outward Horizontal Thrust." The opponent's action can be detected because he is within view of your peripheral limits.

66a and b - is a good example of a "Front Upward Vertical Thrust." As you will note, the restraining hold of the rear opponent has no bearing in preventing you from using your kick to block the action of your forward opponent.

67a and b - demonstrates how the right knee can be used to crisscross and thwart the efforts of your opponent's right kicking knee. This is an example of a "Front Upward-Inward Diagonal Thrust".

68a and b - demonstrates how the left knee can be effectively used when executing a "Side Upward-Outward Diagonal Thrust." Note that the left hand is in position to check your opponent's other retaliatory efforts.

69a and **b** - a good example of how the leg can still be effective even when you are forced to the ground. Although the above photos demonstrate a "Side Upward-Outward Diagonal Thrust" that can be employed to block an opponent's punch, the legs can readily be converted into devastating strikes.

ORGANIZATIONAL CHART ON PARRYING BLOCKS
(FOOT & LEG)

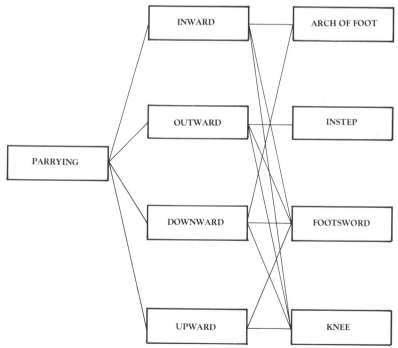

The following photo sequence demonstrates an Inward Parry with the arch of the foot, and an immediate follow-up with a side kick to the stomach of your opponent located in front of you.

Photos **71 a** thru **d** demonstrate the use of the footsword as an Outward Parry while you are on your back.

Some of the foot parries listed on chart C-9 on page 67 can only work when you are on the ground.

Photos 72 a thru d demonstrate the footsword used to parry your opponent's attacking arm in an "upward" and "vertical" manner.

a

b

c

d

Be conscious of using your hands and arms to check further action or a weapon (such as the illustrated flying club) that may get out of control.

ORGANIZATIONAL CHART ON POSITIONED BLOCKS
(FOOT & LEG)

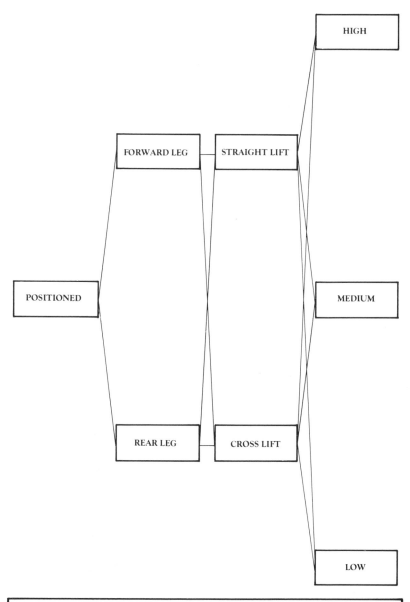

SPECIAL NOTE: Various leg and arm positions may be formed while you are on the ground -- either facing up or down, sitting, kneeling or in a prone position. Depending upon circumstances, these defensive and/or offensive positions can be altered at will to suit the situation.

73 - A High Straight Lift using the forward leg.

74 - A High Cross Lift using the forward leg.

75 - A High Straight Lift using the rear leg.

CHAPTER 4
STRIKES

STRIKES are all *offensive moves* used to *hit* the *vital areas* of an opponent's body. They are basically missile-type moves -- moves that are explosive and accelerate like a projectile to make heavy or light contact. Depending upon the situation, contact may have various effects. It can cause temporary paralysis, injury, inflict pain, or --under extreme cases -- maim, cripple, blind, or kill. These moves can follow linear as well as circular paths employing various parts of the *arms, legs,* or *head.*

There are several *types* of **STRIKES** as well as *methods* of *executing* them (this also applies to **STRIKING BLOCKS**). Application is contingent upon the opportunities that are available both from the standpoint of a *target* and a *natural weapon.* Naturally, if opportunities do not present themselves, deceptive gestures can be employed to create opportunities using *BODY* or *FOOT MANEUVERS.* Nevertheless, if a specific *target* is accessible on an opponent, simple logic would dictate that your choice of a *natural weapon* should be the one closest to the *target* or the *natural weapon* that can render the greatest effect. When the latter is employed, it is generally preceded by a detaining maneuver to allow you time to follow the more time consuming path. It is your overall and engrained knowledge of *types* and *methods* of **STRIKES** that will determine an instantaneous response.

Types of **STRIKES** refers to the *natural weapons* used as you kick, punch, butt, etc. *Methods of executing* them refers to the specific *kind of force* and/or *path, direction* and *position* used in *hitting* your opponent. For example, *butting* is a *hammering method* used to **STRIKE** with the head. Or, you may employ a *thrusting* action with your *fingers,* and thus label it a *finger poke* -- a *thrusting method* using your *fingers.* You may use the *fingers* to *hook, slice,* or *claw* (using several *methods of execution* with the same *type* of *natural weapon*); thus we have the terms *two-finger hook, one finger slice* and *five-finger claw.* A *front inverted thrusting punch* would indicate (1) the *direction* that the *punch* is being thrown (2) the *position* that the *fist* should be in at the time of contact, and (3) that a *thrusting method of force* is being used to execute the *punch*. You may also combine several *methods of execution* into one motion such as a *thrusting claw* which involves a *thrusting motion* ending in a *clawing finger motion*. Other combinations can be a *thrusting action* ending in a *slice*, a *hammering motion* ending in a *thrust*, a *hammering motion* ending in a *claw* and other similar combinations.

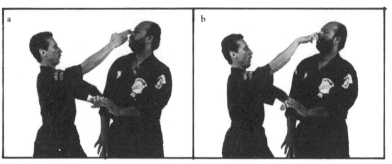

Photos **76a** and **b** are a combination of a Thrust and Slice.   Photos **77a** and **c** combine a Thrust followed by a Five Finger Claw.

Photos **78a** thru **c** are a Hammering motion combined with a Five Finger Claw.

As already indicated, *punching* and *butting* are *types* of **STRIKES**. Although they employ many *methods of execution*, they specifically confine themselves to making contact *with* a *certain part* of the anatomy. For example, *punches* may employ many of the *methods of execution,* but it is only the *front portion of the fist* that makes contact. Should the back of the fist be used (in a back hand motion) it would no longer be labeled a *punch,* but a *back knuckle* **STRIKE**. If, however, the *front of the knuckles* were used (with the same back hand motion) it would then be called a *back knuckle PUNCH.* This may sound confusing, but it will be easier to understand when you read the captions and study the illustrations.

Butting also employs many of the *methods of execution.* It utilizes the head as a *natural weapon.* This is a special weapon that should *not* be used unless all other *natural weapons* fail. Even then, only certain parts of the head should be used to *butt.*

Stomping is yet another *type* of **STRIKE**. It is a special *type* of kick employing the *heel* of the foot. The *HEEL* **KICK**, where the majority of your body weight is placed over and above the action, is primarily delivered below the level of your waist. Although *THRUSTING* is the *method of execution* most generally used, *HAMMERING methods of execution* may also be used.

Regardless of their descriptive terms -- *punching, butting, stomping* -- they are nevertheless classified as **STRIKES**.

There are *seven major methods of executing* **STRIKES**. An eighth category consists of *specialized methods* that deserves a division of its own. The *seven major divisions of* **STRIKES** are *methods* of (1) *THRUSTING,* (2) *WHIPPING,* (3) *HOOKING,* (4) *ROUNDHOUSING,* (5) *SLICING,* (6) *HAMMERING,* (7) *CLAWING. Specialized methods of executing* **STRIKES** include such *methods* as *LIFTING* and *LOOPING.*

Several of the *seven major methods of executing* **STRIKES** have comparable terms that are often used interchangeably. *SNAPPING* is often used instead of *WHIPPING* and *SCOOPING* is sometimes used to describe a *HOOK.* The terms *CRESCENT* or *WHEEL* may be used to describe *ROUNDHOUSE* kicking techniques. *SLICING* techniques using the hands have related terms such as *RAKING* and *GLANCING.* When the feet are employed, the term *SHOVEL* is used. Although each appears to be different, they are identical in principle. A *SNAP* occurs as a result of a *WHIP* and a *SCOOP* is a *HOOK* that follows a vertical plane in a reverse motion. Inspite of the fact that the aforementioned terms are interrelated, I have only listed the more commonly used. Remember, comparable terms will be used in describing *methods of execution* associated with specific *natural weapons* other than those listed. Be sure to study, learn and use them as part of your Martial Art's vocabulary.

Specialized **STRIKES** are often by-products of the *seven major methods of execution.* For instance a *thrusting punch,* missing its *target,* could, without a loss of motion, be converted into a *lifting forearm* **STRIKE** (see photos 79a thru c on page 77). A *thrusting back kick* could immediately be converted into a *stiff leg lifting kick* employing an entirely different part of the *leg* to **STRIKE** with (see photos 80a thru c on page 77). In other cases, *specialized* **STRIKES** deserve *descriptive* terms of their own because they are like, yet often unlike, the *seven major methods of execution.* A case in point is the *overhead looping* **STRIKE** which boarders on a *roundhouse* or *hook* in combination with that of a *hammering* method. (See photos 81a thru e on page 78.)

Another fine point exists between a **BLOCK** and a **STRIKE**. Although the difference is only a fine line, a **BLOCK** can easily be labeled a **STRIKE** if injury is sustained. Therefore, it can be said that a **BLOCK** becomes a **STRIKE** when pain is inflicted. When this occurs, defense and offense become one; thus changing an *embryonic* move to one of *sophistication.*

81a

b

c

d

e

STRIKES, however, do not include *biting, squeezing, grabbing, choking, buckling, tripping, throwing, ripping, tearing, pulling, pushing, shoving, nudging, joint twisting, locking, jerking, etc.* These are *methods* that often accompany **STRIKES** -- prior, during, or after they are executed. They are personifications or accentuations of a **STRIKE** employed to increase the effect of your actions. See chapter V on page 169 to learn more about these *specialized moves and methods.*

ORGANIZATIONAL CHART ON STRIKES

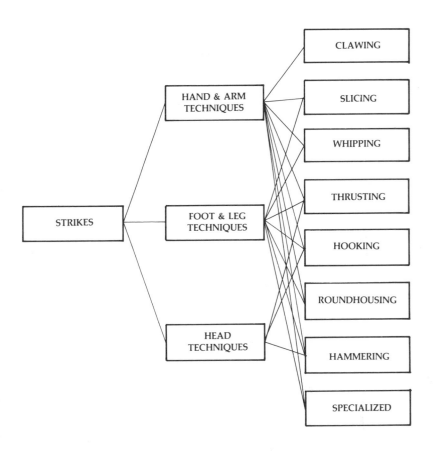

SPECIAL NOTE

It would be a monumentous task to describe each of the **STRIKING** *methods* in detail. Therefore, only a selected number of significant *strikes* will be detailed in this and subsequent chapters. *Self-defense techniques* discussed in Volume V also offers explicit descriptions.

The following charts list the types of strikes that exist. They indicate the countless number of variables that can be chosen from as possible solutions to a variety of situations.

ORGANIZATIONAL CHART ON CLAWING
(HAND & ARM)

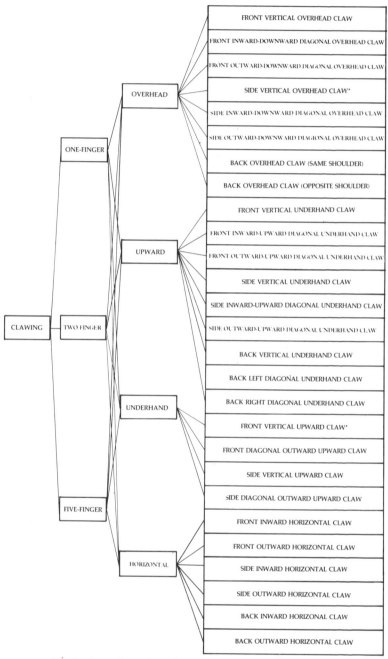

FRONT VERTICAL OVERHEAD CLAW

FRONT INWARD-DOWNWARD DIAGONAL OVERHEAD CLAW

FRONT OUTWARD-DOWNWARD DIAGONAL OVERHEAD CLAW

SIDE VERTICAL OVERHEAD CLAW*

SIDE INWARD-DOWNWARD DIAGONAL OVERHEAD CLAW

SIDE OUTWARD-DOWNWARD DIAGONAL OVERHEAD CLAW

BACK OVERHEAD CLAW (SAME SHOULDER)

BACK OVERHEAD CLAW (OPPOSITE SHOULDER)

FRONT VERTICAL UNDERHAND CLAW

FRONT INWARD-UPWARD DIAGONAL UNDERHAND CLAW

FRONT OUTWARD-UPWARD DIAGONAL UNDERHAND CLAW

SIDE VERTICAL UNDERHAND CLAW

SIDE INWARD-UPWARD DIAGONAL UNDERHAND CLAW

SIDE OUTWARD-UPWARD DIAGONAL UNDERHAND CLAW

BACK VERTICAL UNDERHAND CLAW

BACK LEFT DIAGONAL UNDERHAND CLAW

BACK RIGHT DIAGONAL UNDERHAND CLAW

FRONT VERTICAL UPWARD CLAW*

FRONT DIAGONAL OUTWARD UPWARD CLAW

SIDE VERTICAL UPWARD CLAW

SIDE DIAGONAL OUTWARD UPWARD CLAW

FRONT INWARD HORIZONTAL CLAW

FRONT OUTWARD HORIZONTAL CLAW

SIDE INWARD HORIZONTAL CLAW

SIDE OUTWARD HORIZONTAL CLAW

BACK INWARD HORIZONAL CLAW

BACK OUTWARD HORIZONTAL CLAW

OVERHEAD

UPWARD

UNDERHAND

HORIZONTAL

ONE-FINGER

TWO-FINGER

FIVE-FINGER

CLAWING

Two hands may be used simultaneously or concurrently to execute
DOUBLE CLAWS.

82 - A Front Vertical Overhead Claw

83 - A Front Inward-Downward Diagonal Overhead Claw

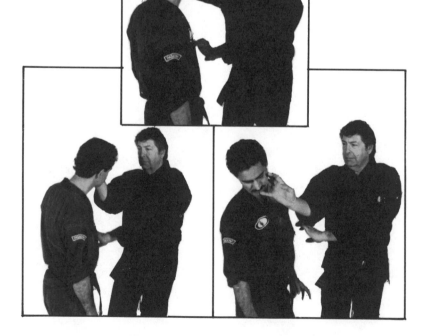

84 - A Front Inward Horizontal Claw

85 - A Front Inward-Upward Diagonal Underhand Claw

86 - A Front Vertical Upward Claw

87 - A Front Outward-Upward Diagonal Underhand Claw.

Photos **88a** thru **d** demonstrate a Back Outward Upward Diagonal Underhand Claw.

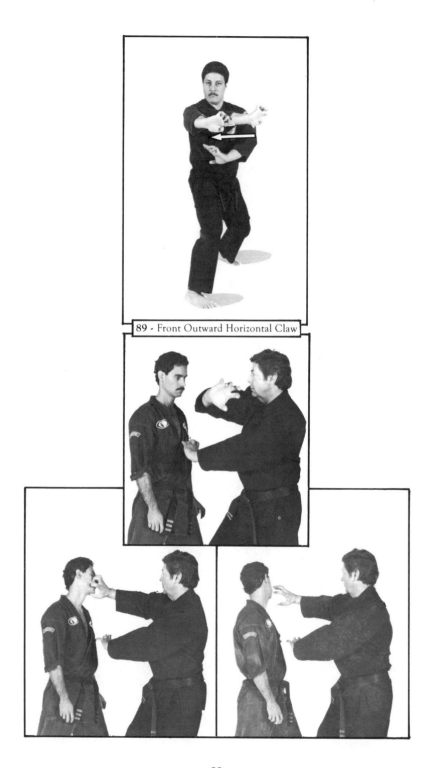

89 - Front Outward Horizontal Claw

90 - A Front Outward-Downward Diagonal Overhead Claw

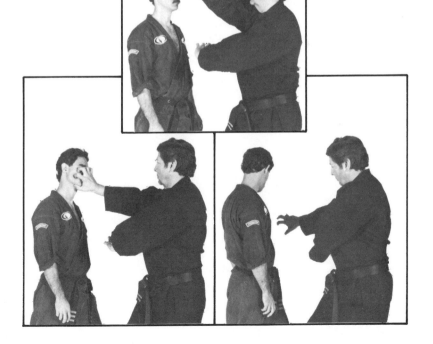

91a thru c - demonstrates a Rear Over-The-Shoulder Claw. This claw is only effective when executed over your opposite shoulder. Clawing to the rear over the same shoulder is very awkward and, therefore, not advised. Whipping over the same shoulder, however, is permissible.

A HELPFUL REMINDER:

The same angles and paths used to execute the various methods of clawing can be duplicated by substituting other natural weapons. The heel of the palm, back knuckle, hammerfist or front of the knuckles can very easily follow the same angles and paths without hampering efficiency and effectiveness.

ORGANIZATIONAL CHART ON SLICING
(HAND & ARM)

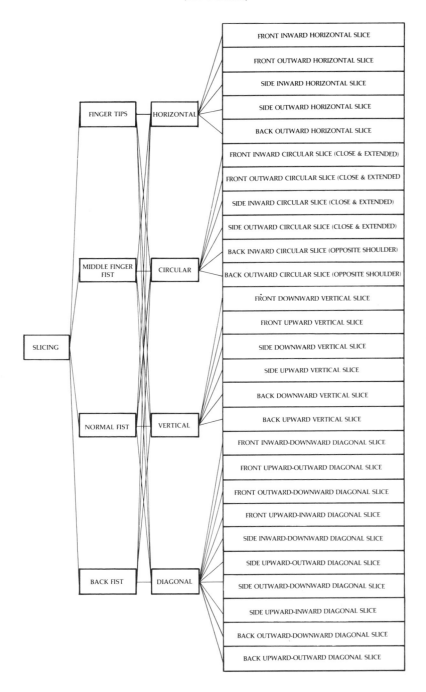

SLICING

FINGER TIPS

HORIZONTAL

FRONT INWARD HORIZONTAL SLICE

FRONT OUTWARD HORIZONTAL SLICE

SIDE INWARD HORIZONTAL SLICE

SIDE OUTWARD HORIZONTAL SLICE

BACK OUTWARD HORIZONTAL SLICE

FRONT INWARD CIRCULAR SLICE (CLOSE & EXTENDED)

FRONT OUTWARD CIRCULAR SLICE (CLOSE & EXTENDED)

SIDE INWARD CIRCULAR SLICE (CLOSE & EXTENDED)

SIDE OUTWARD CIRCULAR SLICE (CLOSE & EXTENDED)

BACK INWARD CIRCULAR SLICE (OPPOSITE SHOULDER)

BACK OUTWARD CIRCULAR SLICE (OPPOSITE SHOULDER)

MIDDLE FINGER FIST

CIRCULAR

FRONT DOWNWARD VERTICAL SLICE

FRONT UPWARD VERTICAL SLICE

SIDE DOWNWARD VERTICAL SLICE

SIDE UPWARD VERTICAL SLICE

BACK DOWNWARD VERTICAL SLICE

BACK UPWARD VERTICAL SLICE

NORMAL FIST

VERTICAL

FRONT INWARD-DOWNWARD DIAGONAL SLICE

FRONT UPWARD-OUTWARD DIAGONAL SLICE

FRONT OUTWARD-DOWNWARD DIAGONAL SLICE

FRONT UPWARD-INWARD DIAGONAL SLICE

SIDE INWARD-DOWNWARD DIAGONAL SLICE

SIDE UPWARD-OUTWARD DIAGONAL SLICE

SIDE OUTWARD-DOWNWARD DIAGONAL SLICE

SIDE UPWARD-INWARD DIAGONAL SLICE

BACK OUTWARD-DOWNWARD DIAGONAL SLICE

BACK UPWARD-OUTWARD DIAGONAL SLICE

BACK FIST

DIAGONAL

92 a thru c - illustrates a Front Inward Horizontal Slice (with two fingers).

b   c

93 a thru c - illustrates a Front Outward Horizontal Slice (with two fingers).

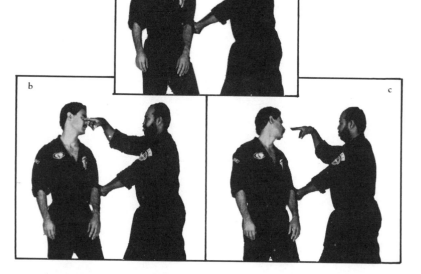

b   c

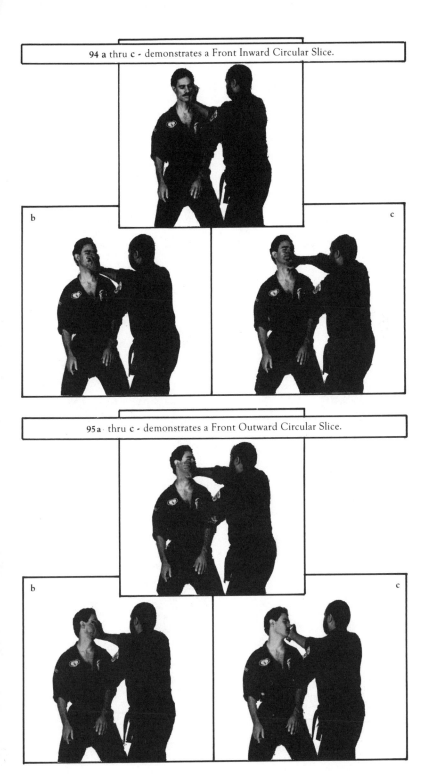

94 a thru **c** - demonstrates a Front Inward Circular Slice.

b

c

95 a thru **c** - demonstrates a Front Outward Circular Slice.

b

c

96a thru d - show the use of a Middle Finger Fist to complete a Front Downward Vertical Slice. 97 a thru d - illustrate a Front Inward-Downward Diagonal Slice with the knuckles.

ORGANIZATIONAL CHART ON WHIPPING
(HAND & ARM)

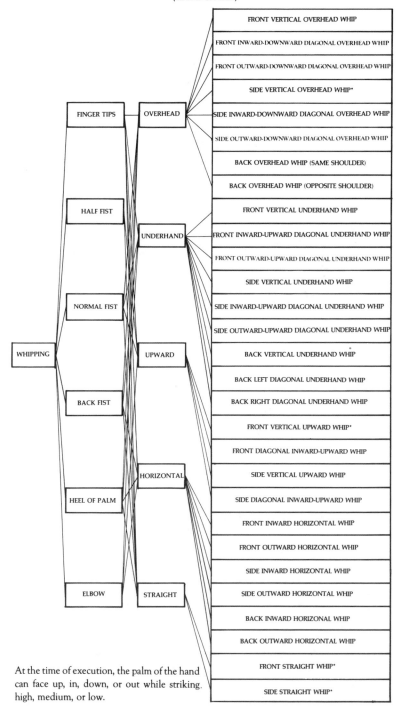

FRONT VERTICAL OVERHEAD WHIP

FRONT INWARD-DOWNWARD DIAGONAL OVERHEAD WHIP

FRONT OUTWARD-DOWNWARD DIAGONAL OVERHEAD WHIP

SIDE VERTICAL OVERHEAD WHIP*

SIDE INWARD-DOWNWARD DIAGONAL OVERHEAD WHIP

SIDE OUTWARD-DOWNWARD DIAGONAL OVERHEAD WHIP

BACK OVERHEAD WHIP (SAME SHOULDER)

BACK OVERHEAD WHIP (OPPOSITE SHOULDER)

FRONT VERTICAL UNDERHAND WHIP

FRONT INWARD-UPWARD DIAGONAL UNDERHAND WHIP

FRONT OUTWARD-UPWARD DIAGONAL UNDERHAND WHIP

SIDE VERTICAL UNDERHAND WHIP

SIDE INWARD-UPWARD DIAGONAL UNDERHAND WHIP

SIDE OUTWARD-UPWARD DIAGONAL UNDERHAND WHIP

BACK VERTICAL UNDERHAND WHIP

BACK LEFT DIAGONAL UNDERHAND WHIP

BACK RIGHT DIAGONAL UNDERHAND WHIP

FRONT VERTICAL UPWARD WHIP*

FRONT DIAGONAL INWARD-UPWARD WHIP

SIDE VERTICAL UPWARD WHIP

SIDE DIAGONAL INWARD-UPWARD WHIP

FRONT INWARD HORIZONTAL WHIP

FRONT OUTWARD HORIZONTAL WHIP

SIDE INWARD HORIZONTAL WHIP

SIDE OUTWARD HORIZONTAL WHIP

BACK INWARD HORIZONAL WHIP

BACK OUTWARD HORIZONTAL WHIP

FRONT STRAIGHT WHIP*

SIDE STRAIGHT WHIP*

WHIPPING

FINGER TIPS

HALF FIST

NORMAL FIST

BACK FIST

HEEL OF PALM

ELBOW

OVERHEAD

UNDERHAND

UPWARD

HORIZONTAL

STRAIGHT

At the time of execution, the palm of the hand can face up, in, down, or out while striking. high, medium, or low.

98a thru **c** - demonstrate a Front Vertical Overhead Whip.

b

c

99a thru **c** - demonstrate a Back Overhead Whip over the same shoulder.

b

c

ORGANIZATIONAL CHART ON THRUSTING
(HAND & ARM)

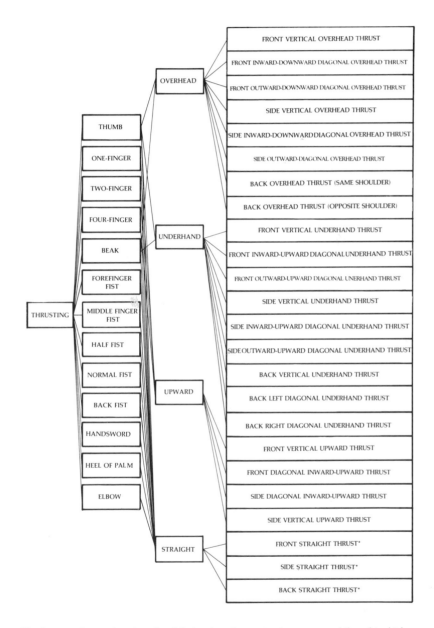

*At the time of execution, the palm of the hand can face up, in, down, or out while striking high, medium, or low.

118a thru **c** - A Front Four-Finger Vertical Overhead Thrust

119a thru **c** - A Back Overhead Thrust (Opposite Shoulder)

98

120a thru **c** - A Front Vertical
Underhand Thrust (With Thumbs)

121a thru **c** - A Front Vertical
Upward Thrust (With Fist)

122a and **b** - A Front Straight Thrust to your opponent's throat using the Half Fist. Notice how the left hand remains on the opponent's left shoulder to keep his action in check.

123a and **b** - A Front Straight Thrust to opponent's solar plexus using the Normal Fist. Again take notice of how the left hand is used to check the opponent's right arm.

124a thru d - A Front Vertical Upward Thrust to opponent's throat using the Handsword. If you will notice, a Sliding Check is applied when the Handsword is executed. Checks are an intergral part of Kenpo training.

125a and b - A Side Vertical Upward Thrust to your opponent's jaw using a Back Elbow Strike. When striking high with one arm, the other arm should be positioned at a lower level to be used as a Check if needed.

ORGANIZATIONAL CHART ON HOOKING
(HAND & ARM)

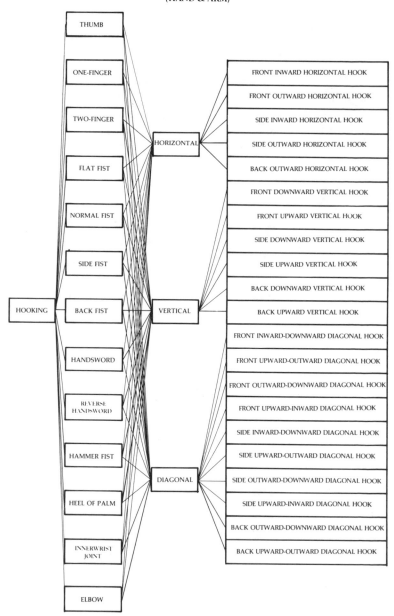

126a thru d - illustrates a Two-Finger Front Inward Horizontal Hook. The left hand is in a position to check further action. An immediate follow-up can be executed by using a right

knee to the groin and a right Inward Elbow Strike to the left side of your opponent's jaw.

127a thru d - A Front Upward Vertical Hook

128a thru d - A Front Inward-Downward Diagonal Hook

ORGANIZATIONAL CHART ON ROUNDHOUSING
(HAND & ARM)

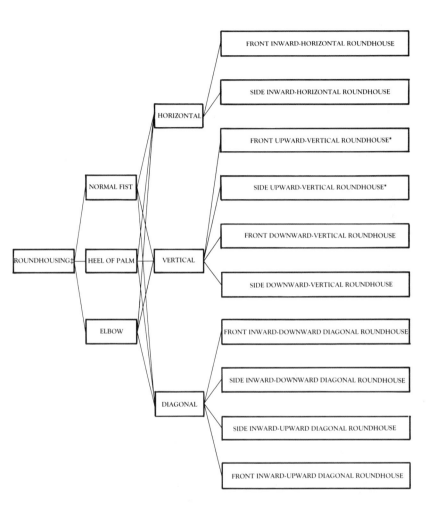

‡ Remember a *roundhouse* makes contact before reaching the apex of a circle. When contact is made after reaching the apex of a circle it is considered a *hook*.

° *Although called an uppercut* punch in the boxing circles it is technically, in principle, an upward *roundhouse* punch that is executed vertically.

† When employed, the normal fist can be placed in a horizontal (palm up or down), vertical (palm in), or inverted vertical (palm out) position. See illustrations on page 168.

105

129a thru d - A Front Inward Horizontal Roundhouse Punch

130a thru c - A Front Upward Vertical Roundhouse (Commonly known as the Uppercut Punch.)

131a thru c - A Side Upward Vertical Roundhouse employing the back of the elbow.

132a thru c - A Front Inward-Upward Diagonal Roundhouse using the heel of the palm.

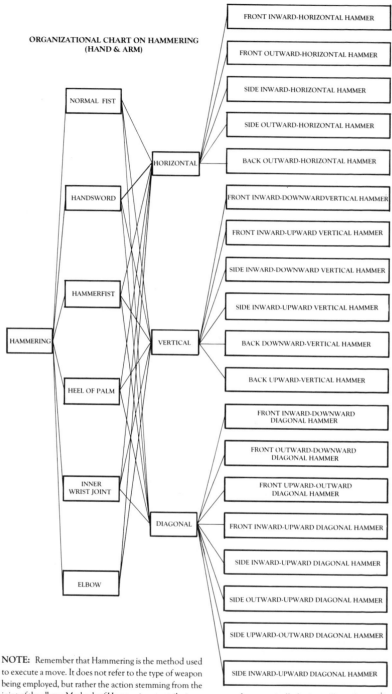

ORGANIZATIONAL CHART ON HAMMERING
(HAND & ARM)

NORMAL FIST

HANDSWORD

HAMMERFIST

HAMMERING

HEEL OF PALM

INNER
WRIST JOINT

ELBOW

HORIZONTAL

VERTICAL

DIAGONAL

FRONT INWARD-HORIZONTAL HAMMER

FRONT OUTWARD-HORIZONTAL HAMMER

SIDE INWARD-HORIZONTAL HAMMER

SIDE OUTWARD-HORIZONTAL HAMMER

BACK OUTWARD-HORIZONTAL HAMMER

FRONT INWARD-DOWNWARDVERTICAL HAMMER

FRONT INWARD-UPWARD VERTICAL HAMMER

SIDE INWARD-DOWNWARD VERTICAL HAMMER

SIDE INWARD-UPWARD VERTICAL HAMMER

BACK DOWNWARD-VERTICAL HAMMER

BACK UPWARD-VERTICAL HAMMER

FRONT INWARD-DOWNWARD
DIAGONAL HAMMER

FRONT OUTWARD-DOWNWARD
DIAGONAL HAMMER

FRONT UPWARD-OUTWARD
DIAGONAL HAMMER

FRONT INWARD-UPWARD DIAGONAL HAMMER

SIDE INWARD-UPWARD DIAGONAL HAMMER

SIDE OUTWARD-UPWARD DIAGONAL HAMMER

SIDE UPWARD-OUTWARD DIAGONAL HAMMER

SIDE INWARD-UPWARD DIAGONAL HAMMER

NOTE: Remember that Hammering is the method used
to execute a move. It does not refer to the type of weapon
being employed, but rather the action stemming from the
joint of the elbow. Methods of Hammering can strike in or out, up or down, vertically, horizontally, or diagonally
using various parts of the anatomy.

133a thru c - A Front Inward-Downward Vertical Hammer using the knife-edge of the hand.

134a thru c - A Front Inward-Upward Vertical Hammer using the back of the fist.

135a thru c - Another version of a Front Inward-Upward Vertical Hammer using the heel of the palm.

136a thru c - A Front Inward-Downward Diagonal Hammer while ironically using the Hammerfist.

137a thru c - A Front Upward-Outward Diagonal Hammer, again using the Hammerfist.

138a thru c - A Side Upward-Outward Diagonal Hammer while stepping in with a Rear Crossover with a Reverse Handsword.

ORGANIZATIONAL CHART ON SPECIALIZED STRIKES
(HAND & ARM)

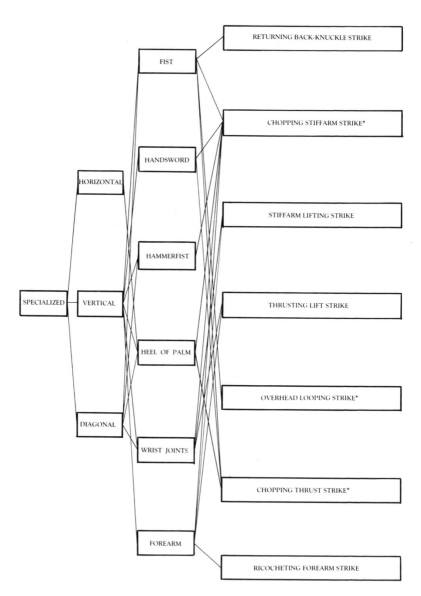

NOTE: The above specialized strikes touch on the majority of those methods of applications used in Kenpo. There are others that are too difficult to describe in writing, but could be demonstrated via film or video cassette tapes.

139a thru f - A Returning Back-Knuckle Strike

140a thru **c** - A Chopping Stiff Arm Strike. It is the shoulder joint that the move hinges off from.

141a thru **c (on the accompanying page)** - demonstrates a Stiffarm Lifting Strike. This strike basically stems from an intended Straight Thrust to the jaw using the fist. The jaw, however, is moved. Therfore, knowing that the original plan has been thwarted, the action unhesitatingly and undisturbingly converts into a Forearm Strike changing from a horizontal to a vertical direction. The flow of action remains constant and the effect is equally as successful.

142a thru **c** - is an example of a Hammering method that instantly converts into a Thrusting method, thus creating a Chopping Thrust Strike. As in the case of the Stiffarm Lifting Strike, the flow of action is undisturbed during the conversion.

A COMPARATIVE ANALYSIS OF
THE ARMS AND LEGS

The *hands* and *arms* are the most versatile of all the *natural weapons*. Because of the support the legs render, combined with the flexibility of the arms and waist, the upper torso is more versatile. For this reason a number of systems place greater emphasis on hand and arm techniques. However, since the *feet* can be a great advantage in combat, they are important weapons. Therefore, with practice, one can intensify the performance of his feet and legs as effective *natural weapons*.

Before discussing the advantages of feet and leg techniques, it would be best if we first analyze their disadvantages. As in other learning skills, to understand and overcome disadvantages often aids in increasing the advantages.

The biggest disadvantage in learning to kick is a natural inability to maintain your balance. With the exception of flying and jumping kicks, one leg must remain on the ground to support the weight of your body while the other leg kicks. Even with experience, balance can be further hampered by uneven, muddy, or icy terrain; floors that are soapy, sandy, powdery, greasy, or oily; or by other hazardous encumberances. The proper weight distribution during the execution of a kick, resistance to shock at the time of contact, and depth penetration are other factors to consider if balance and a firm footing is to be maintained.

While you are kicking, scientific laws must be implemented. Every move must adhere to these laws if the desired effect is to be realized. To be assured of this, balance on the supporting leg must remain constant during every stage of your action. While your balance is shifted, the supporting leg is the vehicle that transfers the weight of the body to the target. If your balance is maintained and the maneuver is swift, body momentum will then enhance this body weight transfe⁻ and thus proportionately increase the impact.

The second disadvantage of kicking relates to speed. The feet are definitely not as fast as the hands. Since the legs are bulky in comparison, they are not easily moved with speed unless training in stretching and limbering the muscles and joints is consistent. Then too, bulk not only hinders speed, it can add to being obvious when employed. Because of the angle of execution plus the size of the leg, it can easily be spotted. The slower speed and bulkiness can therefore cause your opponent to grab your kicking leg and end your hopes of victory. Through proper training, speed and confidence in using the leg will not only increase, but teach you to kick out at a high speed and retrieve the foot at an even faster speed to prevent your leg from being caught.

A third disadvantage can be height. If a kick is delivered too high, that is above a specified level, (depending upon your limberness) power can begin to diminish from that level on up. Interestingly, the strength of a kick is proportionate with the stretching ability of the muscles as they exert maximum power. Your efforts would be wasted beyond this point. Also, speed is curtailed the farther the foot has to travel. Naturally, the closer the foot is to the target prior to executing the kick, the greater the advantage.

A fourth disadvantage, if you're not careful while kicking, can be exposing important vital targets. Kicking high can overly expose your groin area, knee, shin, or if the kick overshoots its mark, vital areas of the back -- kidneys, ribs, spine, etc. -- and become enticing targets for your adversary. Therefore, precautionary measures are recommended while kicking. Make sure that you protect yourself while delivering a kick.

Looking from the positive side, a kick has many advantages. The leg has not only length and reach, but it possesses greater strength than any other limb of the body. Thus, overcoming poor balance and a lack of speed will greatly enhance power. Since kicks are five times more powerful than using the arms, it stands to reason that we should devote concentrated effort to insuring maximum benefit from our kicks. Of course, the length of your leg is a definite asset when you are confronted by an opponent with extremely long arms. Remember, however, that there is also greater advantage if the kicks are kept low since too much height can lessen the effectiveness of your kicks as well as allow for unwarranted exposure. It is always best, especially if you are short, to kick no higher than the solar plexus -- instep, shin, knee, groin, etc. Besides, reacting to lower kicks often compels an opponent to bend to a more desirable level. It is at this time that a second kick could be delivered to the opponent's head, throat, sternum, or other available targets. It certainly makes better sense to lower the height of your major target to a level that will be beneficially effective. Set-up kicks have always proven to be advantageous.

To further understand the relationship of the arms and legs as weapons, we should examine their similarities in usage as weapons as well as the underlying principles that govern them. A typical example is the knife-edge of the hand and the foot. Striking horizontally to the side with the knife-edge of the hand is often called an outward "chop".

Delivering a knife-edge kick to the side is also a "chop", with one difference -- the side of the foot is used instead. Technically then, if you can "chop" with the hand, you can certainly "chop" with the foot. Again, in principle, there is no difference other than the weapon employed. See illustrations.

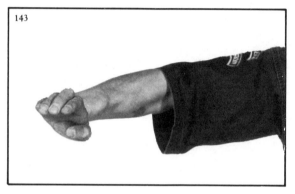

143 - illustrates a Handsword. When employed, it is often referred to as being a Chop.

144 - illustrates a Footsword. Both Handsword and Footsword, when executed, are methods of Chopping. The principles applied to both are identical.

A discussion of similarities is only beneficial if one can detect parallels in principle. If you thoroughly understand a principle when you are employing the arm, but cannot perceive that this principle also parallels the leg, your education of the Martial Arts is destined to take the long route to enlightenment. An example of identical principle can be found when comparing the wrist and ankle. Instruction about the proper method of executing a punch, stresses placing the wrist perfectly straight -- horizontally, vertically, and diagonally. The reason the wrist should be properly positioned at the time of striking the target is to absorb the shock of the impact without injury to the wrist. Any position to the contrary could end in a sprained or broken wrist. Likewise, this same principle should be applied to the ankle, for *the ankle is literally the wrist of the foot.* To position the foot incorrectly might also mean injury to the ankle. Therefore, kicking with the ball of the foot, especially while thrusting with it, the ankle should be kept straight. See illustrations.

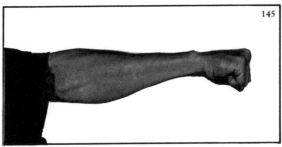

Just as you keep the wrist straight when punching (145) so must you keep the ankle straight when kicking (146). The ankle is literally the wrist of the foot and whatever principle applies to the wrist so should it apply to the ankle.

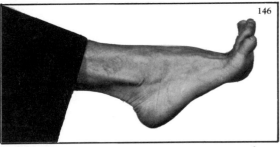

Use logic if you are ever compelled to use your natural weapons. Do not look upon your legs or arms as merely weapons. Natural weapons can be injured just as easily as they injure. In fact, boxing gloves were created for this very purpose. Contrary to what many believe, gloves were not developed to decrease injury to an opponent, but to protect the hands of the fighter. Protecting the hands meant that the matches could be lengthened. Longer matches meant a substantial increase in revenue to both the promoter and the fighter.

Utilizing self-defense implies protecting ourselves from injury. We should, therefore, consider all possibility of injury to ourselves. Precaution should also include protecting ourselves from injury when we are countering. To avoid injury to ourselves entails these considerations: (1) proper positioning of the natural weapon to securely fortify it during the time of contact, (2) properly selecting the target to prevent the wrong weapon from hitting the wrong target, (3) using the proper angle of execution when delivering an attack to insure the proper angle of incident thus avoiding improper angle contact, (4) anticipating your opponent shifting his defensive posture to avoid striking the wrong target, and (5) anticipating your opponent's counters which can partially paralyze or injure you (this can be deterred by the target you select, the angle of execution, and the speed of your action).

Again, use logic when practicing the various ways in which you can employ the arms and legs as weapons. Avoid fancy moves that are impractical. Many of them may look pretty, but are far from functional. Such moves belong on the movie screen and are not practical for real combat. In other words, do not live in a world of Martial Art fantasy. When you are confronted with restrictions, analyze and try to overcome them. If these restrictions cannot be totally overcome, at least know the extent of your limitations. Remember, practice is often the key to pushing to the very limit of your ability. Since kicking is more limited in its use than using the arms, greater effort will be required to overcome the restrictions. However, you'll be amazed at what can be done with consistent practice. Make a concerted effort to practice regularly.

IMPORTANT REMINDERS

Please *do not* look upon **STRIKES** as only weapons of destruction. They can be injured just as easily as they injure. I repeat -- your **STRIKES** are not indestructible, they can also be injured. Therefore, think of your natural weapons as targets as well and this will reduce the possibility of your being an open prey. It must be remembered that when a man is occupied with his own injury, he is not apt to think of retaliation.

Also remember to remain relaxed when blocking or striking. Tense only at the time of contact, then relax again.

CONCEPT OF MINOR AND
MAJOR MOVES

Emphasis on *major* as well as *minor* moves is vitally important. When employing this concept, *minor* moves (those that do not require a great deal of force to execute) are utilized to deflect, deter, detain, distract, deceive, or set-up an opponent's action(s) so that *major* moves (those utilizing concentrated force and power) have a clear passage to your selected target. While *minor* moves are not expected to hurt, *major* moves are designated for that specific purpose. *Minor* moves often contribute to the successful completion of *major* moves.

Boxing is a good example. A left jab is a *minor* move that is often used to set-up a *major* move such as a right cross or a right hook. The left jab serves as a distraction -- a strategic move used to occupy time and space. The right cross or hook is used as an unexpected maneuver that will hopefully knock out or hurt an opponent. Without the use of *minor* moves, *major* moves can be potentially hazardous.

This concept is not only restricted to offensive moves; it can also be employed defensively. The *double factor* concept (where the returning action of one block acts as a temporary safeguard during the execution of the opposite or blocking arm) incorporates the *minor-major* concept. These two concepts employ identical principles. The temporary block which acts as a safeguard is in fact a *minor* block that can also double as a set-up for a *major* block. In this case the *major* block is not intended to hurt, but is used as the principle block for a successful defense.

The *double factor* concept takes advantage of "reverse motion" -- an often overlooked facet of Martial Art's training. Once recognizing the value of "reverse motion" as an interim defense, its use can then be converted into offensive disciplines.

As you observe 147a thru g on the following two pages, the first defensive move (147b) is a Right Outward Parry (minor move) followed by a (147c) Right Inward Blocking Strike (major move) then picked up again (147d) by a Left Outward Parry (minor move) as the right foot chambers for a kick.

a

b

c

d

147e demonstrates the right foot in motion. **147f** shows the kick (major move) striking your opponent's groin, followed by a right Hell of Palm Thrust (another major move) to your opponent's chin. Please observe the intermittent use of major and minor moves, of reverse and opposite motion and the free hand that is constantly available as a Check.

e

f

g

DETERMINING FACTORS

There are several factors that determine the type of kicks you choose, or may be compelled to use during combat. The three primary factors are (1) direction, (2) range or distance, and (3) foot and body positions.

Direction entails knowing where your opponent is located in relation to you. You must instantly determine the angle of your opponent's approach. Is his action stemming from the front, side (left or right), or rear? To be more specific, is he approaching from 12 o'clock, 4 o'clock, etc? The next obvious question is the range your opponent is from you. Range refers to the distance your opponent is away from you in terms of the direction in which he is located. When analyzing range or distance, two view points must be considered -- yours and your opponent's. Position encompasses the location of your feet, which foot is forward or back, and the posture of your body (the structural formation of your body) as well as the direction that you are facing at the time of action. The position of your opponent must also be considered.

Studying feet and body positions cannot be overemphasized. Being conscious of where your feet are located in relation to your opponent's helps you to properly gauge and regulate the range of your kicks. Kicking with your lead leg or rear leg can determine whether your kicks will be jammed or not.

Study of feet and body positions in relation to the direction and distance of your opponent's feet and body positions helps to make you aware of exposed areas (on both you and your opponent) that may or may not exist. There are at least 28 notable possibilities that your feet and body can be found in when approached from four of the major directions -- 12 o'clock, 3 o'clock, 6 o'clock, and 9 o'clock. (45 degree angle approaches would naturally add to the number of possibilities.)

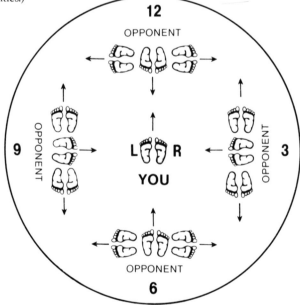

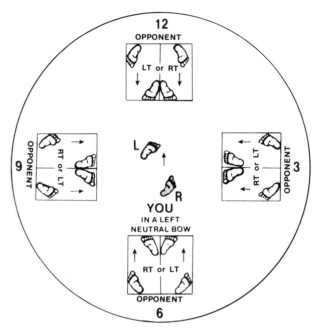

There are only four ways you can face an opponent -- left to left (your left foot opposite your opponent's left foot), left to right (your left foot opposite your opponent's right foot), right to right (your right foot opposite your opponent's right foot), and right to left (your right foot opposite your opponent's left foot). Other positions are variations of those just mentioned.

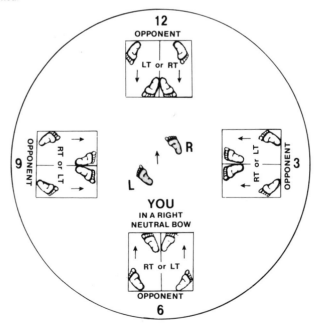

Just a simple step with your lead or rear foot can alter the direction that you are facing so that 3, 6 and 9 o'clock could automatically become 12 o'clock. This works well, especially when you are exposed from either the flank or from the rear. This in no way implies that a suitable counter could not be activated from the position you may be in at the time. Many effective counters can stem from these positions before changing directions. It is just that directional changes helps to diminish unwarranted exposure.

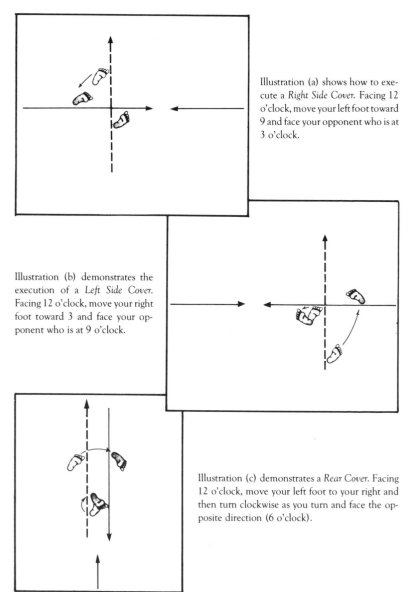

Illustration (a) shows how to execute a *Right Side Cover*. Facing 12 o'clock, move your left foot toward 9 and face your opponent who is at 3 o'clock.

Illustration (b) demonstrates the execution of a *Left Side Cover*. Facing 12 o'clock, move your right foot toward 3 and face your opponent who is at 9 o'clock.

Illustration (c) demonstrates a *Rear Cover*. Facing 12 o'clock, move your left foot to your right and then turn clockwise as you turn and face the opposite direction (6 o'clock).

ORGANIZATIONAL CHART ON SLICING (GLANCING)
(FOOT & LEG)

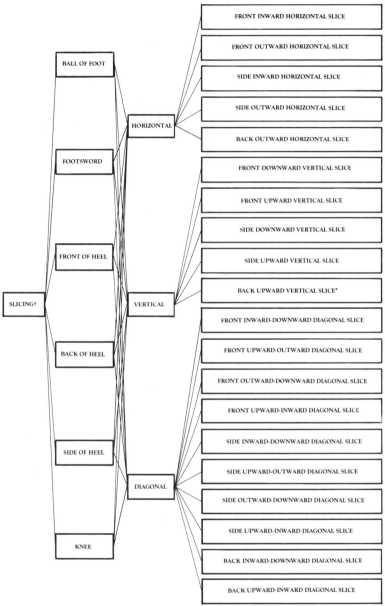

NOTE: The effectiveness of the above weapons would depend upon both your and your opponent's postural positions at the time they are employed.

* Different than hand & arm techniques because of the type of weapon employed, an upward action is much more effective when employing the legs. Again this would depend on the position an opponent is in -- standing, kneeeling, on hands and knees, on stomach or back.

† Glancing or raking are other terms often used to describe slicing.

The above sequence (**148a** thru **d**) is an example of a Front Inward Horizontal Slice utilizing the knife-edge (Footsword) of the right foot. Delivery is executed on an opponent that is on his feet.

The above sequence (**149a** thru **d**) is another example of a Front Inward Horizontal Slice using the knife-edge of the foot. The kick, however, is delivered to an opponent who has been forced onto his knees.

150a thru **d** - demonstrates a Front Upward Vertical Slice. This kick is executed on an opponent who has been dropped on his knees.

151a thru **d** - shows how a Front Upward Vertical Slice can be applied when you are caught on your back.

152a thru **d** - demonstrates a Front Inward-Downward Diagonal Slice utilizing the knife-edge of the foot.

ORGANIZATIONAL CHART ON WHIPPING (SNAPPING)
(FOOT & LEG)

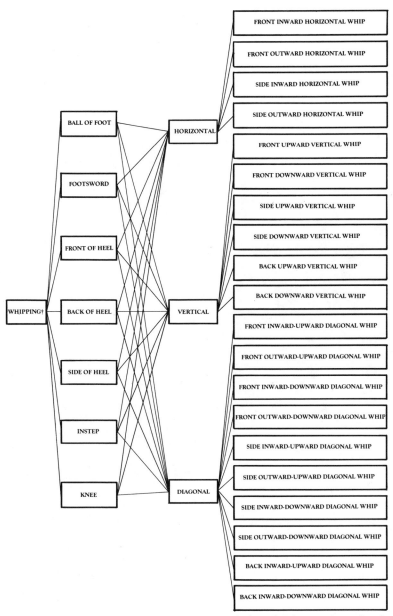

NOTE: The above chart outlines the more common methods used. Others may be employed, but here again it would largely depend upon your and/or your opponent's postural positions. As to what choice would be rendered.

† Stomping is another term that describes thrusting.

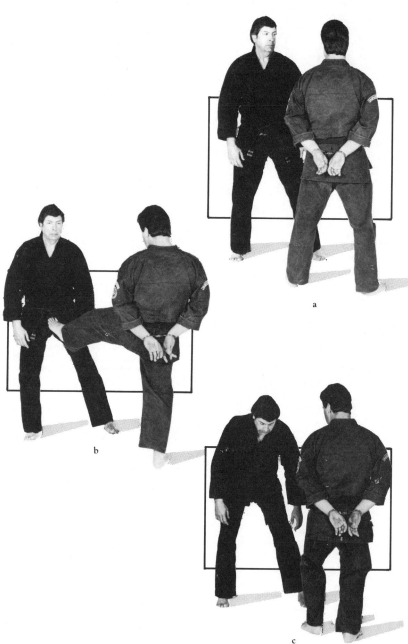

153a thru c - depicts the use of a Front Upward Vertical Whip (Snap) where the retrieving speed of the kicking foot is slightly faster than the delivered speed. This is true of all Whipping type strikes. Notice the hands at a disadvantage since they are handcuffed.

a

b

c

d

154a thru d - illustrates a Side Outward Horizontal Whip (Snap). Observe the left hand that is chambered for further action.

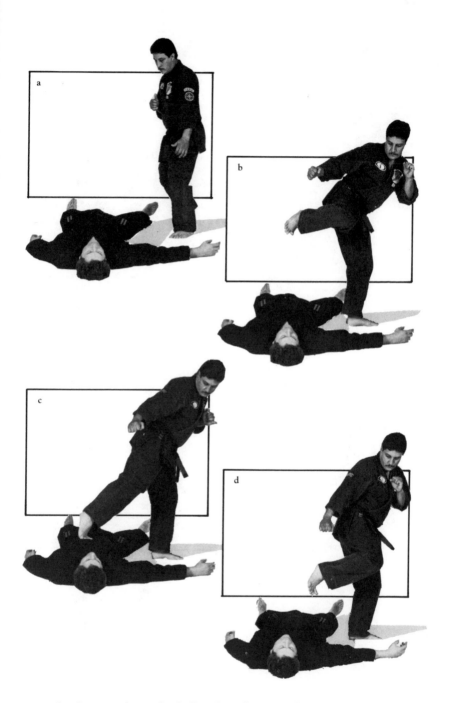

155a thru **d** - is a good example of a Front Inward-Downward Diagonal Whip (Snap).

ORGANIZATIONAL CHART ON THRUSTING (STOMPING)
(FOOT & LEG)

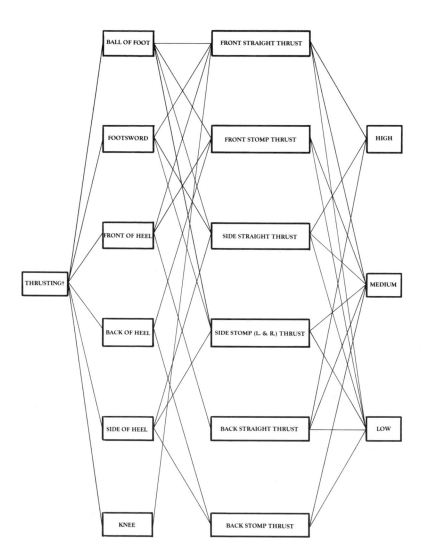

NOTE: The above chart outlines the more common methods used. Others may be employed, but here again it would largely depend upon your and/or your opponent's postural positions. As to what choice would be rendered.

† Stomping is another term that describes thrusting.

156a thru c - A High Front Straight Thrust (to chin)

157a and b - A Medium (height) Front Straight Thrust (to solar plexus)

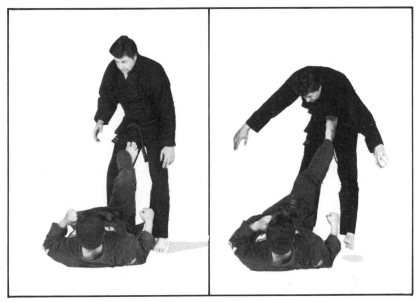

158a and **b** - demonstrates a High Front Straight Thrust to the opponent's solar plexus while delivering a kick from the ground. Remember, you can defend as well as attack while you are positioned on the ground.

159a and **b** - demonstrates a Low Front Stomp Thrust Kick to the solar plexus of an opponent who has been forced on his back. Immediate follow-up maneuvers are required at this point to limit unwarranted exposure.

160a - with your opponent on his hands and knees...

160b - proceed to do a left Rear Crossover Foot Maneuver toward your opponent and...

160c - execute a medium height Right Back Straight Thrust Kick using the front portion of the right heel of your foot. Counter balance your weight by properly adjusting the positions of your arms during each transitional weight change.

161a thru c - A Left Side Stomp Thrust Kick

162a and b - A Right Back Straight Thrust Kick

ANGLE OF NO RETURN

One can never be considered too cautious if he instantly maintains a strategic position after delivering a kick. This is especially true if your upper body travels beyond the *angle of no return*. The *angle of no return* refers to the position and angle of the upper body (and hips) while delivering a front kick (a forward motion), making it awkward, difficult, and illogical to attempt to return to your starting position. (See illustrations.) Because of the awkwardness and the time needed to return to your original position, exposure of your vital areas would work in your opponent's favor -- not to mention your inability to render an immediate counter.

If you are positioned in an *angle of no return*, it is suggested that you adhere to at least one of these two alternatives, (1) step forward while following up with a counter (using an arm or leg), or with your arms structurally positioned in a safe defensive posture, and (2) immediately plant your kicking leg into a front crossover (foot maneuver) so that you can instantaneously cover out to create distance between you and your opponent. This strategy will place you in a position of readiness as you anticipate the next encounter. (See illustrations.)

Through consistant practice you will discover that, *slicing, thrusting, hooking,* and *roundhouse* type kicks (directed to the front) require pivoting the upper body and hips beyond the *angle of no return* to achieve maximum power. Utilize the suggested alternatives to complete your kicks safely and still allow yourself to be in a state of readiness.

163 - illustrates the imaginary line that your upper torso can come up to and which would still make it feasible to drop back to your original "point of origin" without unwarranted exposure.

164 - illustrates the body going beyond the "angle of no return". Any attempt to return to your "point of origin" would place you in danger of unnecessary exposure.

With your right foot back (**165a**), proceed to cock your right foot as you come up to the "angle of no return" (**165b**). Your upper torso at this point parallels the "angle of no return".

You now have two choices. You can execute a Front Straight Thrust Kick as demonstrated in 165c, and return to your point of origin without too much difficulty and exposure, or you may extend your kick beyond the "angle of no return" (165d). When number two is chosen, either punch after the kick, execute a Front Crossover Reverse, or do both.

ORGANIZATIONAL CHART ON HOOKING
(FOOT & LEG)

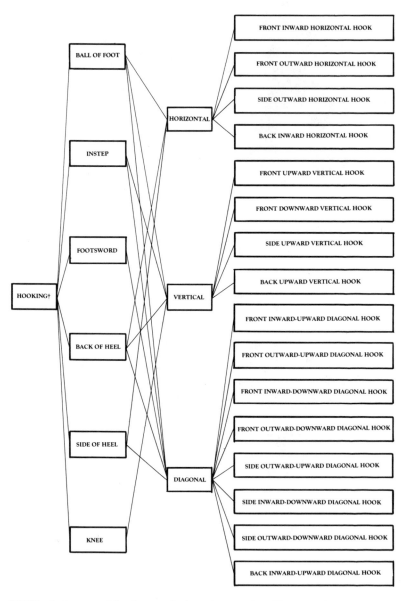

NOTE: Again many of the above methods can be more favorably executed depending upon both your and your opponent's postural position at the time of employment.

† Snapping is another term used for whipping.

The above sequence (**166a** thru **d**) is an excellent example of a Right Front Outward Horizontal Hook Kick.

FRONT SCOOP KICK

Although a **FRONT SCOOP KICK** is not as effective as many other kicks, it nevertheless is an excellent *minor* move which allows you time to execute a kick (hand or arm strike) of *major* significance. When it is delivered correctly, the effect of a **FRONT SCOOP KICK** could be compared with a bucket of ice water that is unexpectedly thrown on you during a 120° heat wave. The drastic change in temperature is substantial enough to take your breath. During this brief period, your body is in a state of suspension. The same effect can be achieved if an opponent is the recipient of a **FRONT SCOOP KICK** to the testicles. He would also be in a brief period of immobility. During this period you can take advantage by following up with a *major* counter. Again, the importance of *minor* moves can never be overemphasized. It is vital to combat.

A **FRONT SCOOP KICK** is actually a Vertical Hook Kick -- that is, contact is made after passing the apex of your circle. When contact is made on the return or downside of a circle, it is labled a Hook. When contact is made prior to the apex of the circle, or on the upside of a circle, it is called a *Roundhouse*.

167a thru e - illustrates a Front Upward Vertical Hook Kick using the instep to strike with.

Please observe the position of the left hand in the above photos. As previously discussed, such positions are known as Positioned Checks. Also observe the chambered right hand that is prepared for a follow-up.

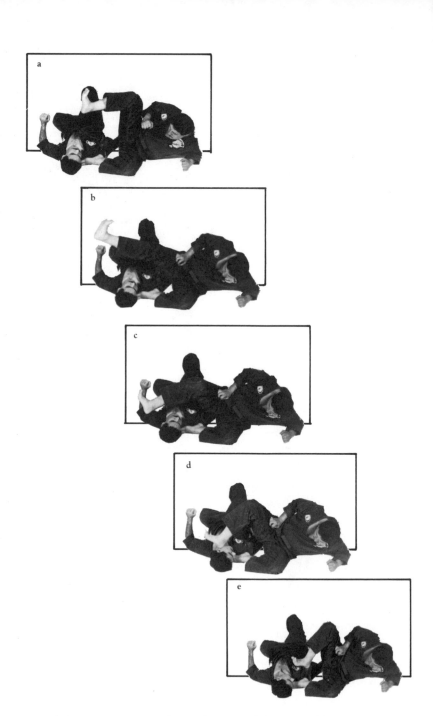

168a thru **e** - A Front Downward Vertical Hook used when you and your opponent are on the ground.

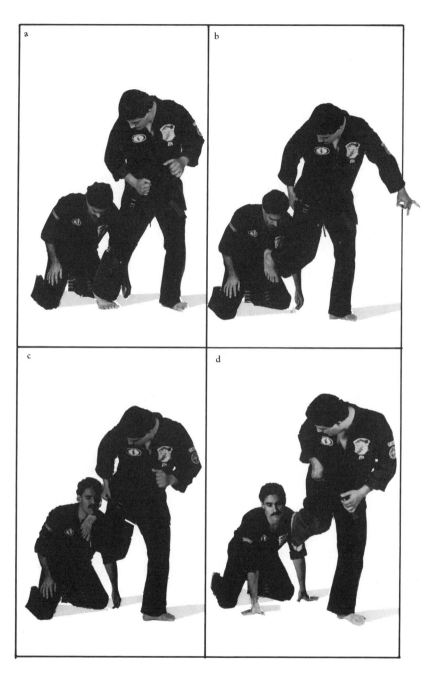

169a thru **d** - illustrates a Back Upward Vertical Hook on an opponent who is on his hands and knees. This kick is also known as a REAR SCOOP KICK.

170a thru **d** - demonstrates a Right Front Inward-Downward Diagonal Hook on an opponent who habitually likes to position his left hand low. When executed properly, the kick will aid in keeping the opponent's Height Zone in check.

ORGANIZATIONAL CHART ON ROUNDHOUSING
(FOOT & LEG)

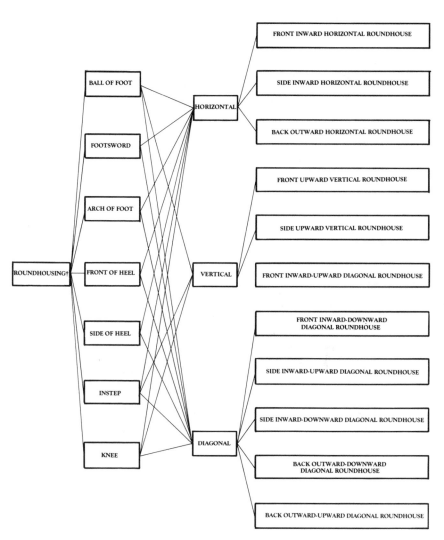

NOTE: The above chart outlines only selected methods commonly used contingent upon your or your opponent's postural positions at the time of employment.

† Crescent or wheel kick are two other terms that are often used to describe a roundhouse kick.

The above sequence (**171a** thru **d**) illustrates a Right Front Inward Horizontal Roundhouse Kick. This kick is very popular at tournaments and has been instrumental in adding points to a competitor's score.

172a thru c - illustrates a Right Front Inward-Upward Diagonal Roundhouse Kick. The instep is used to strike the left side of your opponent's neck.

ORGANIZATIONAL CHART ON HAMMERING
(FOOT & LEG)

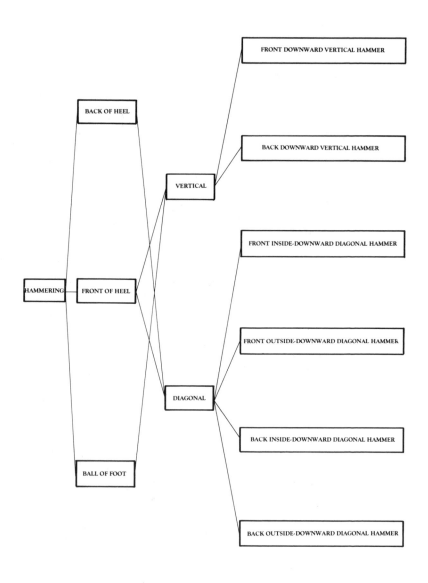

NOTE: The above chart describes those methods used when you are on your knees and your opponent is in a prone position. However, some of the above methods may still be employed while you are standing and your opponent still in a prone position.

The sequence below (**173a** thru **c**) demonstrates a Front Downward Vertical Hammer Kick. The Hammering action stems from the joint of the knee.

The sequence below (**174a** thru **c**) demonstrates a Right Front Outward-Downward Diagonal Hammer Kick.

This photo sequence (175a thru d) illustrates a Right Front Inside-Downward Diagonal Hammer Kick.

ORGANIZATIONAL CHART ON SPECIALIZED KICKS
(FOOT & LEG)

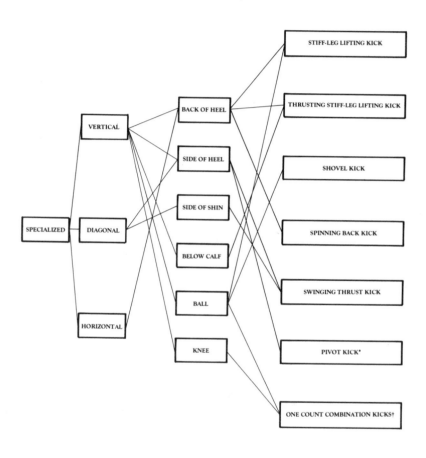

*While pivoting on ball, heel stomp.

† Two or more kicks that make contact in a single movement.

The above sequence (**176a** thru **c**) depicts a Stiff-Leg Lifting Kick where the joint of the hip is the primary pivot point. The leg is stiff from the time of inception.

177a thru **c** - demonstrates a Right Thrusting Stiff-Leg Lifting Kick. The leg first lifts by using the joint of the hip with the right knee slightly bent. Just prior to making contact to the chin, the knee is straightened by Thrusting out and up. The flow of action is one continuous motion.

The above sequence (**178a** thru **c**) illustrates a Shovel Kick. The maneuver resembles the action used while shoveling dirt. During the single action delivery, two targets are struck -- the knee and the ribs.

The above sequence (179a thru d) demonstrates a Spinning Back Kick. Facing your opponent with your left foot forward (179a), spin clockwise (179b) and proceed to kick with your right foot (179c). Use the front of your right heel to kick your opponent's solar plexus (179d).

The above sequence (180a thru c) demonstrates a Right Pivot Kick. While in a Right Cat Stance (180a) violently pivot counterclockwise on the ball of your right foot (180b) and strike your opponent's face with your Right Heel (180c).

ORGANIZATIONAL CHART ON HEAD STRIKES
(HEAD)

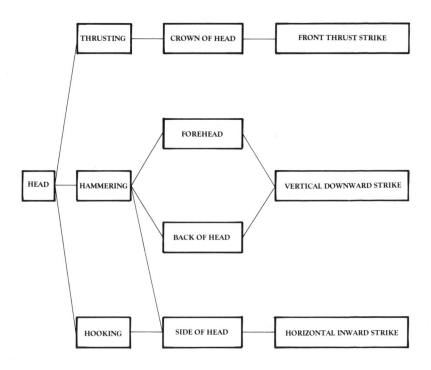

NOTE: The chart above lists the more common head strikes that can be used. Other variations in terms of method and portion of anatomy used as a weapon could be effectively employed. Caution is a must when employing the head as a weapon. Its use must not injure you in the process.

181a and b - A Front Thrust Strike using the Crown of the Head.

182a and b - A Front Vertical Downward Hammer Strike using the Forehead.

183a and b - A Back Vertical Downward Hammer Strike using the Back of the Head.

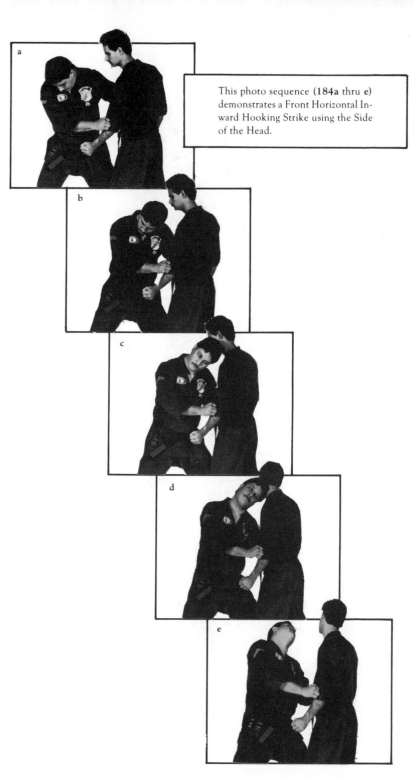

This photo sequence (**184a** thru **e**) demonstrates a Front Horizontal Inward Hooking Strike using the Side of the Head.

It is hoped that the few examples of strikes shown and the methods in which they can be executed and applied will help to make you aware of what the organizational charts contain as well as the multitude of variables that Kenpo offers. We have not even touched on the possible working combinations that can be created with both the hands and the feet. The effective use of functional combination sequences are endless. See Volume V which contains examples of combination possibilities. Remember combinations must be structured so that they stress sequential flow and continuity that economize on motion. See Volume V for a better understanding of MOTION.

While flying and jump kicks are stressed and favored by other stylists, Kenpo practitioners prefer to remain practical in their application of kicks. As is true of any rule, exceptions can occasionally overrule as the only practical alternative where no other will work.

ANOTHER REMINDER

The same angles and paths that the hands and arms travel when striking targets on the upper torso of a standing opponent could easily be substituted by using the feet and legs should an opponent be forced on to his knees. It is faster to strike the upper torso of an opponent with your hands and arms when he is standing and just as expedient to strike with your feet and leg when the upper torso is forced to a lower level. Again, depending on the angle of execution as well as the target, the hands can still be employed effectively even when an opponent is forced to his knees. Versatility as well as knowledge of variables using natural weapons on targets located in a multitude of postural positions is what makes Kenpo unique and all inclusive.

A REPEATED REMINDER

Please *do not* look upon **STRIKES** as only weapons of destruction. They can be injured just as easily as they injure. I repeat -- your **STRIKES** are not indestructable, they can also be injured. Therefore, think of your natural weapons as targets as well and this will reduce the possibility of your being an open prey. It must be remembered that when a man is occupied with his own injury, he is not apt to think of retaliation.

A COMPOSITE OF NATURAL WEAPONS

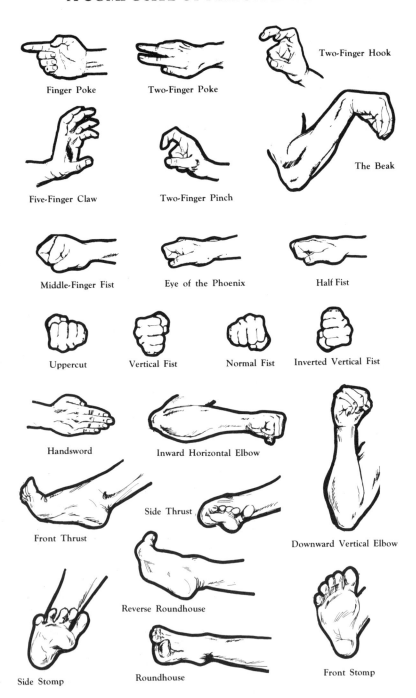

Finger Poke

Two-Finger Poke

Two-Finger Hook

Five-Finger Claw

Two-Finger Pinch

The Beak

Middle-Finger Fist

Eye of the Phoenix

Half Fist

Uppercut

Vertical Fist

Normal Fist

Inverted Vertical Fist

Handsword

Inward Horizontal Elbow

Front Thrust

Side Thrust

Downward Vertical Elbow

Side Stomp

Reverse Roundhouse

Roundhouse

Front Stomp

CHAPTER 5
SPECIALIZED MOVES
AND METHODS

SPECIALIZED MOVES AND METHODS are just that. They are *moves and methods* that are related to those described in the first four divisions of **BASICS**. Since they have distinct characteristics of their own, they are in a category or division apart from the others.

These *moves and methods* can be more clearly understood by subdividing them into logical steps of progression. You will be shown how one subdivision can be constructed or added to another to make learning easier.

The first subdivision is *VICE-LIKE* **MOVES** -- *moves* that compress a particular part or area of an opponent's body. **MOVES** that belong to this subdivision can be executed by *biting, squeezing, pinching, hugging, grabbing, tackling* (which is a running grab), *choking, sandwiching, fulcruming* and *scissoring*.

Follow-up *methods* of *VICE-LIKE* **MOVES** give us our next category -- *PULLING* **MOVES**. After a *grab* or *squeeze* is applied, the **METHODS** of *PULLING* such as *jerks, yanks, rips* and *tears* can be employed on an opponent's clothing, limbs, joints, etc.

PUSHING **MOVES** are our third subdivision. Further subdivisions associated with *PUSHING* are **METHODS** of *pressing, nudging, bumping* and *shoving.* They may be used to create distance, force one opponent into another to delay their action, or to force an opponent off balance (*pulling* can also accomplish this).

The next logical category is *UN-BALANCING* **MOVES** -- **MOVES** that can cause an opponent to loose his balance and enhance your counter moves. These **MOVES** can be employed prior to, during, or after a defense or offense. **MOVES** that are listed under this category are *buckling, tripping, throwing,* and *sweeping.* Some of these subdivisions listed under *VICE-LIKE, PULLING* and *PUSHING,* like **STRIKES,** can be used to force an opponent off balance.

JOINT TWISTING **MOVES** are *specialized* **MOVES** listed in the *SPECIALIZED DIVISION.* These *MOVES* or **METHODS** are used to twist an opponent's joints to cause pain, sprain, dislocate, or fracture and are *specialized* because they combine methods of *PULLING* and *PUSHING.*

Another *SPECIALIZED* **MOVE** is *LOCKING* **MOVES** -- **MOVES** that lock the joints or body parts of your opponent to restrain him from taking further action. Here again *VICE-LIKE* **MOVES** combined with *PULLING* and/or *PUSHING* **METHODS** are the ingredients that make *LOCKING* **MOVES** possible. Therefore, *SPECIALIZED* **MOVES** within each *MAJOR DIVISION* are **MOVES** that are combinations of the various subdivisions.

185 -Twisting

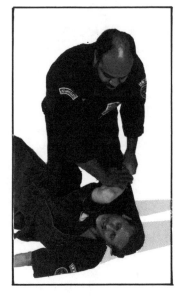

186 - Locking

NOTE: *SPECIALIZED MOVES* listed and described in each of the first four *DIVISIONS* on the *BASICS CHART* are not to be confused with the *DIVISION ON SPECIALIZED MOVES AND METHODS.* *SPECIALIZED MOVES* in the first four *DIVISIONS* generally relate to combined moves within each of the first four *DIVISIONS*. In analyzing the move, it is not just one specific type of move, but combinations of one or more moves within a single action. Therefore, you would not say that it is one type of a move or another, but rather a *specialized move* incorporating several types or methods in a single action -- thus, the need for *SPECIALIZED MOVES* within each of the first four *DIVISIONS* on the *BASICS CHART*.

ORGANIZATIONAL CHART ON
SPECIALIZED MOVES & METHODS

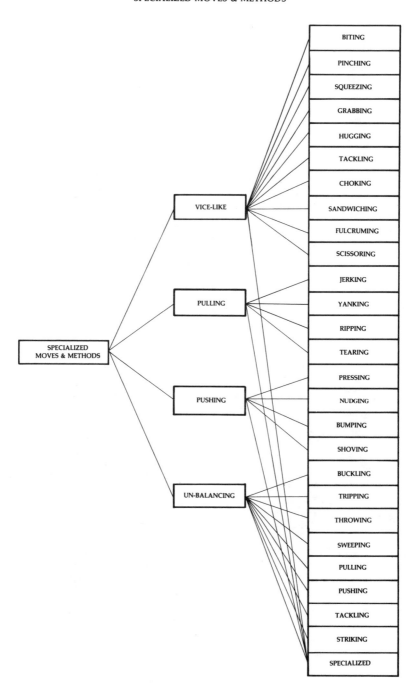

187 - Grabbing

188 - Yanking or Jerking

189 - Pressing

190 - Shoving

191 - Buckling

192 - Tripping

193 - Sweeping

Specialized moves within the basics of Specialized Moves and Methods are numerous, however, those that are noteworthy are described herein.

LOCKS - Involve the simultaneous action of pulling while twisting with a push, strike, or snap. Spraining, dislocating joints, and breaking limbs can result from applying full pressure during the execution of a lock. Locks may employ other body parts as fulcrum and leverage devices simultaneous with the pull, twist, push strike or snap. Locks are refined follow-ups after strikes have been executed.

JOINT TWISTS - are special because pushing, pulling, and turning are needed to make the action work effectively. Joint Twists are partial ingredients that are found within Locks. Depending upon the amount of pressure applied, Joint Twists can result in a sprain or dislocation.

TAKEDOWNS - are throws that are more violently executed, they involve pulling while striking. The opposing force of pulling with a strike causes injury on the onset of the initial action with added injury occurring when the opponent hits the ground.

**ORGANIZATIONAL CHART ON
SPECIALIZED MOVES WITHIN
SPECIALIZED MOVES & METHODS**

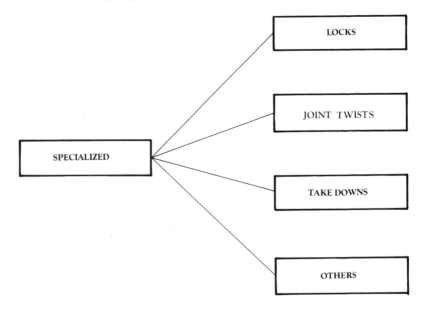

194 - Locks

195 - Twists

196a thru c - Takedowns

AN IMPORTANT REMINDER

Specialized moves and methods described in this chapter are methods that often accompany **STRIKES** (or **BLOCKS**) -- prior, during, or after execution. They are personifications or accentuations of a **STRIKE** (or **BLOCK**) employed to increase the effect of your actions.

ANOTHER IMPORTANT REMINDER

It is of vital importance that you learn every conceivable (but practical) maneuver and method (deceptive or otherwise) to execute your natural weapons. Technical and deceptive use of your natural weapons often gives you the edge. Therefore, knowing your alphabets of motion must also include increasing your vocabulary of motion with all of its ramifications. To have a limited knowledge of your basics is comparable to a carpenter who uses his saw for cutting, drawing a straight line, and also as a hammer. Specific tools used in carpentry enhance your efforts. Likewise, specific methods of using your natural weapons also increase the effectiveness of your efforts. (See illustrations of carpenter using his saw.)

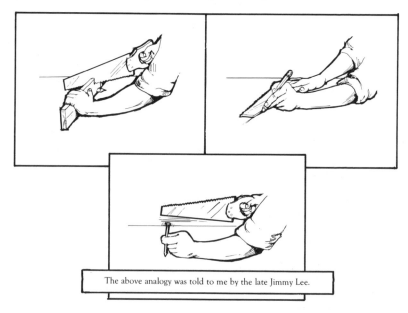

The above analogy was told to me by the late Jimmy Lee.

CHAPTER 6
EXERCISES

PRE-STRETCHING

A lack of flexibility often thwarts the movements of beginning Martial Artists. Although strength and endurance may be developed and maintained with a minimum amount of flexibility, skill depends upon flexibility to increase the effectiveness of conscientious practitioners. Generally thought of as the ability to make anatomical joints move through a normal range or better, flexibility involves three types of movements utilizing the joints of the body: flexion (bending) and extension; rotating in two directions (in or out); abduction versus adduction. While range of motion is a factor that has been widely researched and experimented with, how the joint can easily be moved within the mid-range of motion (where speed is usually the greatest), is a factor needing further study.

Flexibility is basically divided into two classifications: (1) *static* --the measure of range of motion, and (2) *dynamic* -- stiffness of a joint. In either case, it involves a single muscle or group of muscles pulling in one direction while another muscle, or group of muscles pulls in the opposite direction. These contrasting muscles are referred to as antagonists.

Most of today's conventional exercises favor *dynamic flexibility* where the antagonists are stretched by the dynamic movement of the agonist. In other words, one body segment is put into motion to actively contract a muscle or group of muscles which stimulus causes the opposite muscle or group of muscles to relax. This sequence of response is called the *"ballistic method"* and is subject to the Law of Reciprocal Innervation. On the other hand, this same Law achieves the reverse response by first relaxing the muscles that are to be contracted. Since muscles are tight prior to applying them to all types of physical activities, pre-stretching exercises loosen muscle fibers to prepare them for further stretching activities. To elaborate, pre-stretching muscle releases involve holding a *static* position for a short period of time by locking the selected joints into position, which, in turn, automatically and comfortably stretches the muscles to their greatest possible length. Through this *"static method"* of stretching, flexibility is increased by giving stimulus to antagonistic muscles that need to be stretched. As a result, flexibility takes less time to develop. Although pre-stretching before stretching is somewhat of a new precept, its practicality has become more widespread as a result of experiments now being done on accident victims seeking total recovery.

There are three distinct advantages of the *"static method"* over the *"ballistic method"*: (1) there is less danger of overextending the muscle tissues; (2) energy requirements are lower; (3) it relieves muscular soreness and does not cause it.

Pre-stretching exercises require firm, constant, and uninterrupted pressure, not bouncy or jerky movements. Since the stretching of muscle fiber is directly proportionate with the amount and rate of movement that causes the stretch, bouncing brings into play a built in nervous mechanism called the anti-gravity syndrome, which defeats the purpose of the pre-stretching precept. A firm, steady, static stretch invokes the inverse myotonic reflex which brings about inhibition not only of the muscle fiber, but also the tissue surrounding it. Thus, the results of pre-stretching are not only more favorable, but longer lasting.

It must be remembered that pre-stretching exercises are not to be considered the last word in warm-up exercises. They should be done prior to other types of stretching, warm-up, and work-out activities. It is also suggested that they be done immediately after a workout to minimize any stiffness or soreness of muscles and joints.

The following are pre-stretching exercises recommended by Craig L. Weidel, Black Belt and member of the International Kenpo Karate Association as part of his written thesis. He used and also modified some of these exercises as a means of rehabilitating himself after sustaining an injury in a traffic accident. In the concluding remarks of his thesis he states:

"It is best to start using these pre-stretches on beginners because they are usually the most unflexible. You should see immediate change in the person's flexibility especially in the lower extremities. Flexibility after a certain amount of time, becomes a secondary characteristic. The primary characteristic being that of injury prevention through reducing joint and muscle damage."

"There are two final factors that will help a person in making my pre-stretches work for them. The first factor is that extreme caution should be taken while engaging in the pre-stretches. If at anytime during a pre-stretch a person feels any type of pain they should immediately stop and do not try to push it any longer. I would like to remind you that the purpose of the pre-stretches is to loosen the muscle fibers to prepare them to be stretched, and not to injure them in any way. Pain during pre-stretch tells us that the fibers are being microscopically torn and this is not what an individual wants. The second factor is that if a person wants to get full benefit out of the pre-stretches that they must give one-hundred percent effort on each repetition. This insures the person that they are getting into play the majority of all the myofibrils in the muscles. In other words, if you do not give one-hundred percent then you will not loosen all the myofibrils. Because of this, you stand a chance of pulling a muscle during your post-stretching activities."

"I believe that if you use the pre-stretches that you will find that you will make beneficial gains in flexibility. Along with flexibility gains comes the insurance that you may participate in activities without the fear of pulling or tearing muscles or ligaments. Because of these two items I believe you will enjoy and hopefully progress faster in the Martial Arts."

NECK RELEASES

There are three methods that can be utilized to bring about *neck releases*. These methods can be executed while kneeling on both knees and with both arms held in front of your chest. Method *one* is executed by having someone apply downward pressure on top of your head (see illustration). Push up with your head and against the resistance. This releases the muscles in the back of your neck (upper trapezius semispinalis capitis, and splenius). Refer to Volume IV Chapter Five to learn where these muscles are located on the body.

Method *two* releases the muscles on the side of the neck (stenocleidomastoideus, scalenus anteriormedius, and scalenus posterior). See illustrations. This method involves applying pressure to the right side of your head first and then your left. In either case, push out and against the applied pressure. The *third* release involves the muscles that make your head move down (splenius). To put these muscles into play, have someone apply upward pressure from under your chin. Then push down against the applied pressure with your head and chin. Be sure to repeat these releases at least five times each. Make sure that your assistant pushes as hard as he can for five seconds allowing for complete periods of relaxation between repetitions. This policy should apply to all of the following exercises.

SHOULDER AND UPPER-BACK RELEASE

This pre-stretching exercise is designed to release the *shoulder and upper-back* muscles. The main muscles involved are the deltoid trapezius, infraspinatus, levator scapulae, subclavius, and serratus anterior. Kneel on both knees with your arms stretched out toward the floor. Now have an assistant apply downward pressure on both of your wrists (see illustration). Bend both of your arms and shrug your shoulders. Now push up and against the applied pressure. Tense the muscles of the shoulders only. Try to eliminate tensing your arms if at all possible. Do at least five repetitions for a period of five seonds each.

CHEST RELEASES

The following pre-stretching exercises are designed to relax and release the two major chest muscle groups (pectoralis major and minor). Lay flat on your back (on the ground or floor) with both of your arms stretching up and toward the sky. Place both of your palms firmly together. Now have your assistant apply (1) inward pressure against both of your arms as you make every effort to push them out and (2) have your assistant force both of your arms apart as you push in and against the applied pressure. Do five repetitions each, of the two exercises, for a period of five seconds.

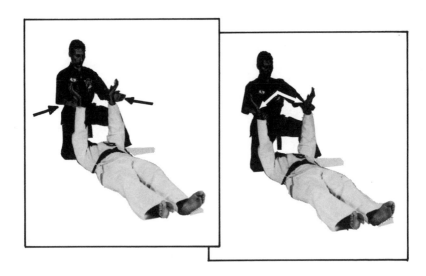

ARM RELEASES

The following two exercises can help the front or back of your arms depending upon which part of your arm you wish to release. While kneeling on both knees, hold your arms in front of your chest and bend your elbows so that the upper and lower portion of your arms are at a forty-five degree angle. The *first* exercise is designed to release the biceps. To accomplish this, have your assistant apply downward pressure on your wrists. As you executed the other exercises, push up and out against the applied pressure as you attempt to straighten your arms. The *second* exercise is designed to release the triceps. The only difference between this and your first exercise is that the pressure is reversed. This is done by having your assistant apply upward pressure from under your wrists as you push down and out in an attempt to straighten your arms. **CAUTION** -- your assistant should not try to lift your arms with his back, but only with his arms. Both exercises should be done five times each for a period of five seconds per repetition.

NECK AND UPPER AND LOWER BACK RELEASES

There are two exercises that can aid the release of the *neck and upper and lower back.* To execute the *first* exercise sit erect and suck your stomach in as you concentrate on elevating your ribs. Once you are properly positioned, rotate the trunk of your body to the right and touch the floor with your left hand. See illustration. Return to the starting position and repeat the same process on the opposite or left side. Executing this exercise will release the interspinales, rotatores, multifidus, latissimus dorsi, serratus anterior and lower trapezius muscles. The *second* exercise also commences from the same seated position. The requirement is that you raise your arms above your head (see illustration) as you look up toward the sky. From this position, rotate your upper body as far to the right as possible. Again return to your original position and repeat this exercise on your left. This exercise will help to release the semispinalis capitis, iliocostalis lumborum, iliocostalis thoracis, iliocostalis cervicis, longissimus thorascis-cervicis-capitis and the spinalis thoracis-cervicis muscles. Both exercises are to be done five times each and are to be held for at least five seconds. Once the rotations are done, you should be able to stretch to the farthest position.

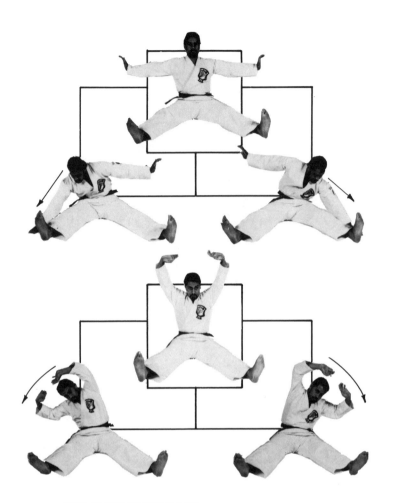

HIP FLEXOR RELEASE

This exercise requires that you lie absolutely flat on your back (see illustration). From this prone position, grab your right knee and pull it up and toward your chest as far as possible. Hold this position for three seconds. Now have your right leg return to the starting position. However, concentrate on stretching your right leg out as far as possible. Relax and repeat the same exercise using your left leg. This exercise will release the psoas major, iliacus, sartorius, rectus femoris, pectineus, tensor fasciae latae, gluteus maximus-medius-minimus, biceps femoris, semitendinosus, semimembranosus, gracilis, adductor magnus, and pubofemoral ligament muscles. Do five repetitions with each leg for a period of three seconds each.

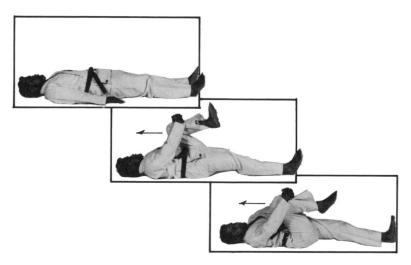

HAMSTRING RELEASE

To execute this exercise, sit on the floor with your legs extended; spread your legs out (keeping your knees straight) while leaning back on your hands (see illustration). With the aid of an assistant, have him apply downward pressure on your right leg with one hand above and the other below your right knee. As your assistant applies downward pressure attempt to raise your right leg off the floor without bending your right knee for a period of five seconds. Relax, and repeat the exercise with your left leg. This releases the semitendinosus, semimembranosus, and biceps femoris muscle group (hamstring). Do each leg separately five times each for a period of five seconds.

ABDUCTOR RELEASE
(Inside of Thighs)

To release the muscles of the inner thigh, lie down, with one leg straight and the other raised but bent (with the foot flat on the ground). See illustration. Have an assistant attempt to push the raised leg down and towards the ground. Counteract the downward pressure by using the muscles of the inner thigh to resist the pressure (in the opposite direction) for a period of three seconds. Now have your assistant extend the flexed leg and cross it over the opposite leg. After propping the leg up in the same manner, repeat the application of pressure for two more three second repetitions. Straighten the leg and repeat the same procedure with the opposite leg. Do at least five repetitions for each leg.

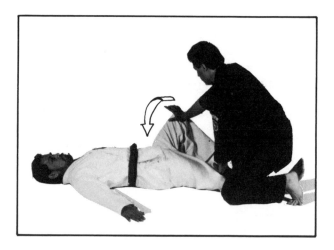

ABDUCTOR RELEASE
(Outside of Thighs)

Sit with your legs together, knees straight and legs extended while leaning back on your hands. Have two assistants apply inward pressure from the outside of your legs. Resist their attempts by forcing your legs apart. As you attempt to spread your legs, keep your outward pressure constant for a period of three seconds. Repeat the process five times for a period of three seconds each.

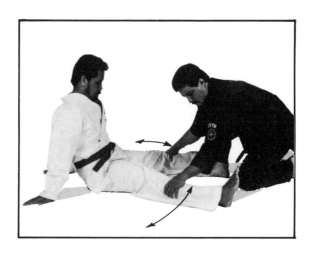

QUADRICER AND HAMSTRING RELEASE

This exercise is to be done after completing the hamstring releases. While this exercise comes in *two* parts, it is considered more of a *static* stretch release. In part *one,* release is obtained by standing on one leg (your supporting leg should be straight) while the other leg is up on a bar or table. To accomplish this exercise, simply lower your head down and toward the leg that is proped on the bar or table. Have your head reach down as far as possible and hold it in that position for at least ten seconds. Straighten up and continue the exercise with the opposite leg. Part *two* is the same except for one additional move. After lowering your head, squat with your supporting leg until a ninety degree squatting position is maintained (see illustration). Remain in this position for ten seconds before straightening up and switching sides. Part *one* relaxes the quadricep group (rectus femoris, vastus lateralis, vastus intermedialis, and vastus medialis). Part *two* exercises the hamstring group (rectus femoris, semimembranosus, and semitendinosus). Each of these stretches should be done five times on either side.

GASTROCNEMIUS AND SOLEUS RELEASE
(Calf)

This exercise is also done in two parts. Part *one* requires that you face and stand parallel to the wall with both heels on the floor and knees straight. Without moving your feet, lean forward and against the wall with your upper body while resting on your hands with your elbows bent (see illustration). This maneuver alone will make you feel the pull on your calf muscles. Part *two* is done by simply bending both of your knees (see illustration). Part *one* releases the gastrocnemius and part *two* the soleus muscles. Each part should be done five times for a duration of four seconds each.

LOWER BACK AND BUTTOCKS RELEASE

Because of the tightness of the lower back muscles, there are many who are unable to touch their knees with their foreheads. This release exercise will help you to loosen these muscles (extensors of the spine intertranversalis, interspinales, rotatores, multifidus, glutaeus medius, and glutaeus maximus). To benefit from this exercise, sit on the floor with your legs extended and spread apart. Make sure your back is straight, your head is erect and both arms are extended in front of your body (see illustration). Have an assistant apply pressure against your chest as you resist being pushed on your back. Press forward with your entire body for a period of five seconds. After each repetition, try to passively touch your knees with your head without using force. Do five repetitions for a period of five seconds each.

OTHER EXERCISES CONDUCIVE TO LEG TRAINING

Once your muscles are released by utilizing pre-stretching exercises, stretching should then be your next consideration. The following exercises should aid you in achieving further flexibility:

Leg Splits

Side to Side Leg Stretches

See-Saw Back and Leg Stretches

Leg Stretch Using the Shoulder **Leg Stretch Using the Hands**

Straight Leg Stretches **Bent Leg Stretches**

Leg Lifts

Back and Leg Stretches

It goes without saying that all body parts should be stretched and limber if a kick is to be fully functional; therefore, do not overlook any of the exercises described herein . The following limbering exercises should help to insure leg and body flexibility.

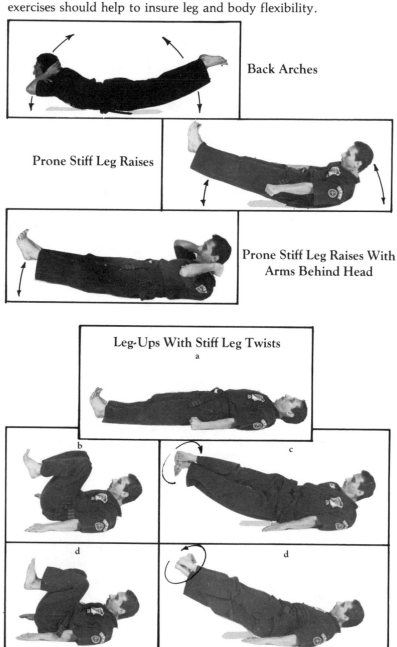

Back Arches

Prone Stiff Leg Raises

Prone Stiff Leg Raises With Arms Behind Head

Leg-Ups With Stiff Leg Twists
a

b

c

d

d

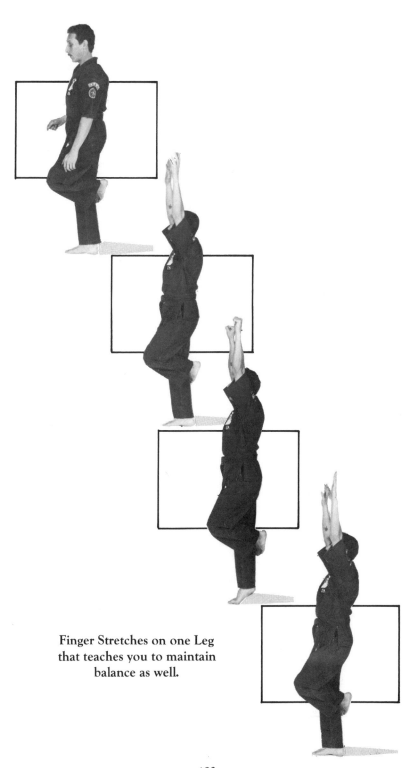

Finger Stretches on one Leg
that teaches you to maintain
balance as well.

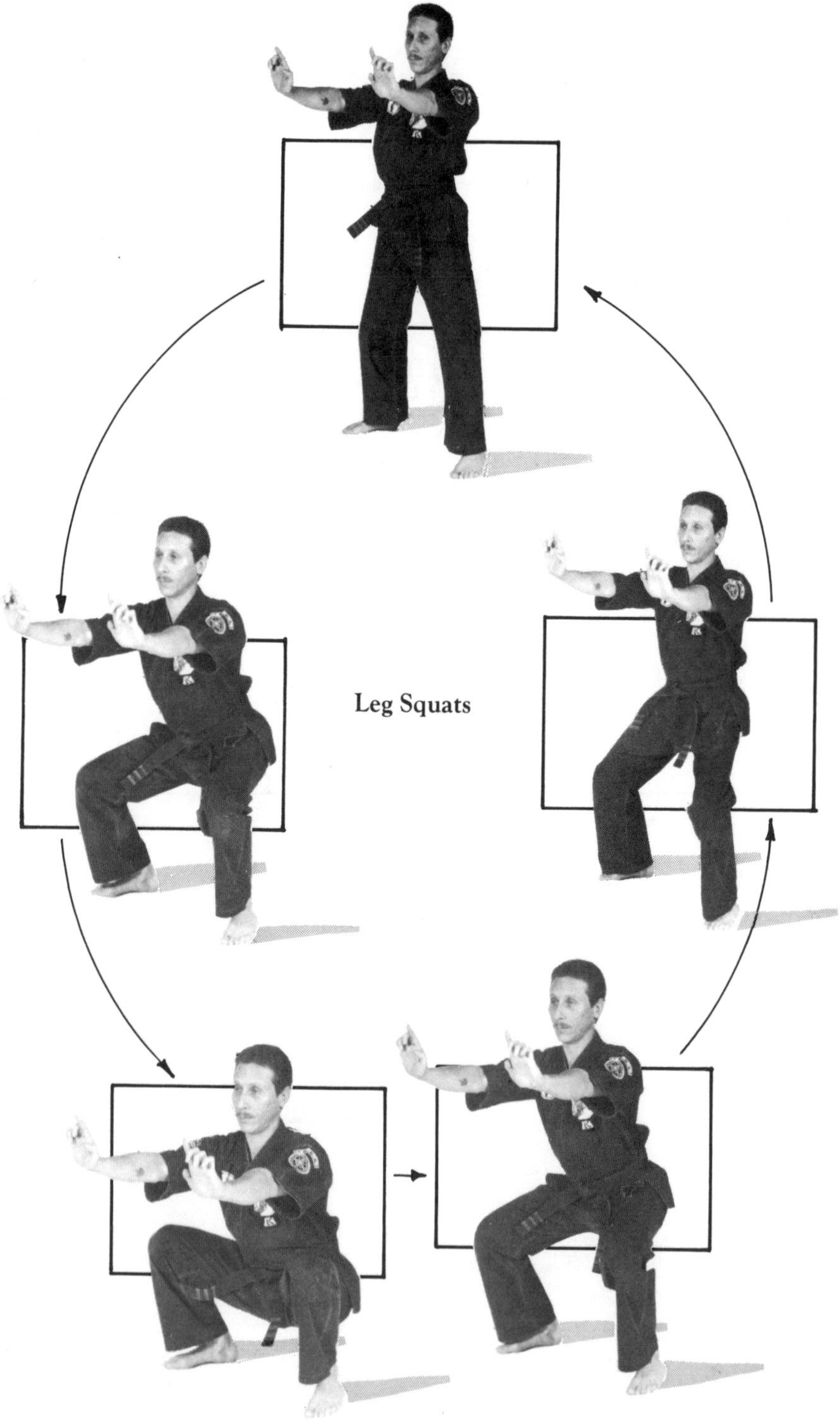

Leg Squats

Now that your legs are limber, let us progress to exercise that will give you the added strength needed for endurance, stamina, and power.

Knuckle Push Ups

Palm-In Push Ups

Finger Push Ups

Sit Ups

Combination Knee Bends and Sit Ups

GOOD TIMBER

The tree that never had to fight
For sun and sky and air and light,
That stood out in the open plain,
And always got its share of rain,
Never became a forest king,
But lived and died a scrubby thing.
The man who never had to toil,
Who never had to win his share,
Of sun and sky and light and air,
Never became a manly man,
But lived and died as he began.
Good timber does not grow in ease;
The stronger wind, the tougher trees.
The farther sky, the greater length;
The more the storm, the more the strength;
By sun and cold, by rain and snows,
In tree or man good timber grows.
Where thickest stands the forest growth,
We find the patriarchs of both,
And they hold converse with the stars
Whose broken branches show the scars
Of many winds and much of strife;
This is the common law of life.

Unknown

CHAPTER 7
CONCLUSION

Volume III concludes the topic of "Physical Analyzation". It, however, in no way eliminates the need to use other constituents that are imperative to maximize the physical movements that have been learned. Knowledge of how to employ the powers of the mind, synchronized breathing, sight, hearing and touch to produce total awareness; the chronological use of balance, timing, speed and power; knowledge of angles, body alignment and targets; a thorough understanding of motion and what it consists of and how it can be used advantageously, is needed to achieve peak performances. (See Volume IV.) To exclude any part of these constituents is to limit your ability to maximize your efforts.

While these constituents provide distinct advantages in your overall make-up of action, knowledge of their application and what they are used for (definition of motion), and what targets render instant benefits are all important prerequisites that add flavor to the flow and effectiveness of your physical efforts. (See Volume V.)

To have a complete knowledge of the Kenpo system does not stop at *how* and *what*, but also includes *why*. The statements found in the introduction of Volume II, "The man who *knows how* will always be a student, but the man who *knows why* will maintain his position as the instructor." and in the introduction of this volume, ..."*know what* you know; *know why* it's so" contains great wisdom. All three -- *how, what* and *why* should be learned. A knowledge of each of these elements makes a complete Martial Artist. This does not mean that you cannot be effective if you only know *how* and *what* because you still can be victorious in combat. Knowing *why* allows you to analyze combat in total. It makes it possible for you to be an engineer of motion capable of blueprinting a logical, updated system compatible with the times. Knowing *why* insures your ability to correct the blueprint of logical and practical thinking. It directs you as to *when* and *why not* do a particular move. Having a total understanding of the concepts and principles associated with the Martial Arts affords you this privilege. It is possible that only those of you who seek to be professionals in the Martial Arts may wish to be concerned with the *why*. That is your choice. Regardless, Volumes I through V offers you insights into all three -- the *how, what* and *why.* Volumes II and III touch on the *how,* Volume IV on the *what* and Volume V on the *why.*

GLOSSARY OF TERMINOLOGY

ANATOMICAL POSITIONING -- Calculated striking of vital targets to force an opponent into preconceived postural positions that will make the next target of your choice readily accessible for a successful follow-up.

ANGLE OF NO RETURN -- Refers to the position and angle of the upper body (and hips) while delivering a front kick (a forward motion), making it awkward, difficult, and illogical to attempt to return to your starting position. Because of the awkwardness and the time needed to return to your original position, exposure of your vital areas would work in your opponent's favor -- not to mention your inability to render an immediate counter.

BASICS -- Simplified moves that comprise the fundamentals of Kenpo. They are divided into stances, maneuvers, blocks, strikes, specialized moves and methods, etc.

BLOCKS -- are primarily defensive moves employing physical contact to check, cushion, deflect, redirect, or stop an offensive move.

CATCHING -- A method of stopping and detaining an opponent's strike or block.

CHECK -- To restrain, hinder, or prevent an opponent from taking action. This is accomplished by pressing, pinning, or hugging an opponent usually at the joints so that it minimizes his leverage and nullifies his action. Positioning your arms and legs in various defensive postures can also keep an opponent from striking you effectively.

CLOSE RANGE ENCOUNTERS -- Action that occurs within elbow and knee distance.

CONTACT PLACEMENTS -- Predetermined knowledge of the targets which you plan to strike using the weapon of your choice.

CRESCENT -- A path of action that can be compared and paralleled to a HOOKING type maneuver.

DEPTH PENETRATION -- The concept of going beyond the point of contact when striking with a weapon.

DIRECTIONAL CHANGE -- The ability to switch or alter directions while keeping the momentum of your body flowing constantly so as not to interrupt the initial motion started.

DOUBLE FACTOR -- It entails utilizing dual movements to defend yourself. These moves can incorporate any combination of blocks, parries, and checks. It also refers to sophisticated moves which are dually defensive and offensive. "Reverse motion" is an intergral part of this concept.

EXTENDED OUTWARD -- A type of block that is delivered out, up, and away from the body. It is a block used at medium range.

GLANCING -- A method of striking that is similar to a slice. The major difference is that the depth of penetration is much greater. It does not skim the surface of the target, but makes a deep penetration.

HAMMERING -- A particular method of striking which resembles the action of a hammer pounding a nail from various angles.

HOOKING -- The execution of a natural weapon that makes contact with its target after passing the apex of the circle in which it travels. In short, contact is made on the downside (or the return) the circle in which your weapon travels.

INSIDE DOWNWARD -- A particular method of blocking below your waist that requires your blocking arm to travel from outside in.

INWARD PARRY -- A blocking method that requires your blocking arm to travel from outside in as it redirects a blow or kick by riding or going with the force.

JAMMING -- A special method of blocking that crowds or forces an opponent's natural weapon back and against his joint to prevent it from moving or functioning. It can also be accomplished by forcing an opponent's limb against other parts of his anatomy.

LOCK-OUT -- It is a type of check that is used to slightly detain the action of your opponent. It involves striking a target with a natural weapon and having the weapon remain on the target for a time before retrieving it.

LOCKS -- moves that lock the joints or body parts of your opponent to restrain him from taking further action. It combines methods of pushing and pulling.

LONG RANGE ENCOUNTERS -- Action that occurs at arm length or the length of a leg.

METHODS OF EXECUTION -- The manner in which a move is executed to insure maximum results. Such moves can follow a direct, dipping, looping, hooking, or roundhouse path.

MINOR/MAJOR CONCEPT -- The concept that a minor move is subordinate and although not devastating, it can cause ample damage and/or delay to allow the execution of a major move to occur. Major moves are strong and positive moves which cause immediate devastation.

OUTSIDE DOWNWARD -- A type of block requiring your blocking arm to travel from inside out. It is used for attacks that are primarily directed to targets below your waist.

OUTWARD PARRY -- A block that travels from inside out as it redirects and rides the force of your opponent's strike.

PARRYING BLOCK -- Blocking moves that redirect, ride and go with the force of your opponent's action.

PINNING BLOCK -- A restraining vice like move to hinder an opponent from taking action.

POSITIONED BLOCK -- The formation of various defensive postures that automatically check incoming action. The structured positions in and of themselves act as checks.

POSTURAL POSITIONS -- Assumed body positions for purposes of defense or offense.

PREDETERMINED LABELING -- Wrongfully believing a person to be what he really isn't which can throw you when action occurs.

PRINCIPLES -- Comprehensive and fundamental rules stemming from theories which through devoted analysis develops into proven characteristics that make them doctrine.

PUSHDOWN BLOCK -- A particular blocking method that uses the heel of the palm to control the opponent's strike that is normally directed to targets below the waist.

RAKING -- The execution of a body weapon in a sweeping manner so that it grazes the target with penetrating force. It involves increasing the depth of your circular path so that your natural weapon gouges the surface of your target. It, too, is similar to a SLICE with two exceptions -- the force is greater and the depth more penetrating. Executed properly a RAKE may employ several parts of a natural weapon so that it produces a corrugated effect when making contact with the target.

REVERSE MOTION -- Returning on the same path of an initiated move.

RICOCHETING BLOCK -- A defensive move that uses the first block to launch into a second block. This term is often interchangeably used with a RICOCHETING BLOCKING STRIKE where a block is built into an aggressive strike.

ROUNDHOUSING -- Any weapon that makes contact with its target before reaching the apex of the circular path in which it is traveling.

SCOOPING -- The execution of a weapon that resembles the dipping motion of a shovel. It is literally a reverse HOOK that is delivered vertically.

SET-UP -- Refers to conditioning your opponent to react in a specific manner so that his response corresponds to your desired strategic plan.

SHOVEL KICK -- A specific method of kicking where the path of the action resembles the dipping motion of a shovel when it is in use. This special kick allows your foot to strike two targets with the same move.

SLICING -- An offensive maneuver whereby the weapon being used skims the surface of the target being struck. This action is normally restricted to using a specific area of your natural weapon where no real depth occurs during contact. However, although the depth is not as penetrating as a RAKE, it is , nevertheless, effective. It is basically a MINOR MOVE that is used to set your opponent up for a MAJOR MOVE.

SLIDING CHECK -- A specialized PINNING BLOCK that travels on an opponent's body by sliding from one leverage point to another. During the course of each slide, constant body contact is maintained so as not to allow for retaliation. This is a form of BODY CONTOURING.

SNAPPING -- A method of execution requiring the natural weapon to strike out and back with greater magnitude than the action of a WHIP.

SPECIALIZED MOVES AND METHODS -- are moves and methods that have distinct characteristics of their own. They are neither blocks or strikes and are, therefore, in a category or division apart from the others.

STOMPING -- A thrusting method using the foot to strike down toward targets located on or near the ground.

STRIKES -- are all offensive moves used to hit the vital areas of an opponent's body.

STRIKING BLOCK -- Any block that bucks or goes against the force of an opponent's strike.

TAILORING -- Fitting moves to your body size, makeup, speed, and strength in order to maximize your physical efforts.

THRUSTING -- A particular method used to propel a strike. It resembles an explosive push type action.

TRAPPING -- Is any strategum designed to CATCH a natural weapon to prevent it from escaping.

UPWARD BLOCKS -- All types of blocks that redirect an attacking weapon up, above, over, out or away from your head.

VERTICAL OUTWARD -- A type of block used for CLOSE RANGE ENCOUNTERS that sends the attacking weapon out and away from you.

WHEEL -- A type of kick resembling and paralleling the path of a ROUNDHOUSE kick.

WHIPPING -- A particular method of execution that employs a SNAPPING type of blow or strike, but with less force than a SNAP.

ZONE OF PROTECTION -- This involves shielding three main zones on your body -- height (or horizontal), width (or vertical) and depth.

SPECIAL NOTE: This GLOSSARY only touches on the terms that are used in KENPO. A more comprehensive book is now being completed by Ed Parker, entitled the "**ENCYCLOPEDIA OF KENPO**". This book will not only define the terms, concepts, theories, and principles of KENPO, but will graphically illustrate many of these terms as well. It is a book worth adding to your Martial Arts Library. LOOK FOR ANNOUNCEMENT OF THE PUBLICATION DATE IF YOU WOULD LIKE TO ACCELERATE YOUR KENPO KNOWLEDGE AND TRAINING.

To order additional copies of ED PARKER'S
INFINITE INSIGHTS INTO KENPO, please
mail your check or money order for $9.95
payable to:

ED PARKER
Post Office Box 595
South Pasadena, California 91030

CALIFORNIA RESIDENTS: Please add 6½ %
sales tax. NO C.O.D. ORDERS WILL BE
ACCEPTED.
ADD $1.25 to cover postage and handling if
you reside in the United States. Add additional
postage for foreign requests.

TO THE READER

The author will be most happy to receive your comments, including criticisms
and suggestions. Noteworthy comments may be included in future editions or
books of this series. If a reply is requested please send all correspondence,
including a Self Addressed Stamped Envelope, to:

ED PARKER
Post Office Box 595
South Pasadena, California 91030

Correct postage is necessary if you wish a reply.